# Agricultural Economics

*Edited by Ifeoluwapo O. Amao*
*and Iyabo B. Adeoye*

Published in London, United Kingdom

IntechOpen

*Supporting open minds since 2005*

Agricultural Economics
http://dx.doi.org/10.5772/intechopen.89903
Edited by Ifeoluwapo O. Amao and Iyabo B. Adeoye

Contributors

Barbara Richter, Linda Bitsch, Jon Hanf, Silva Atoyan, Taras Gagalyuk, Mohammad Jahangir Alam, Ismat Ara Begum, Rezaul Karim Talukder, Mohammad Mizanul Haque Kazal, Iyabo Bosede Adeoye, Chamhuri Siwar, Mohd Khairi Ismail, Muhamad Zahid Muhamad, Md. Sadique Rahman, Debasish Chandra Acharjee, Mustapha Momoh, Caroline Aturu-Aghedo, Nana Usman Bature, Nnaemeka Success Esiobu, Orgu Kenneth Chima, Chukwu Andy Onyema, Onubuogu Gilbert Chinedu



First published in London, United Kingdom, 2021 by IntechOpen
IntechOpen is the global imprint of INTECHOPEN LIMITED, registered in England and Wales, registration number: 11086078, 5 Princes Gate Court, London, SW7 2QJ, United Kingdom
Printed in Croatia

British Library Cataloguing-in-Publication Data
A catalogue record for this book is available from the British Library

Additional hard and PDF copies can be obtained from orders@intechopen.com

Agricultural Economics
Edited by Ifeoluwapo O. Amao and Iyabo B. Adeoye
p. cm.
Print ISBN 978-1-83968-537-8
Online ISBN 978-1-83968-538-5
eBook (PDF) ISBN 978-1-83968-539-2

For EU product safety concerns:
IN TECH d.o.o., Prolaz Marije Krucifikse Kozulić 3, 51000 Rijeka, Croatia, info@intechopen.com or visit our website at intechopen.com.

# Meet the editor

Dr. Ifeoluwapo Oluwaseun Amao has a Ph.D. in Agricultural Economics from the University of Ibadan, Nigeria. She is a Chief Research Officer in the National Horticultural Research Institute, Ibadan, Nigeria, involved in monitoring and impact evaluation of institutional projects. She was the project coordinator of one of the institutional research projects that established innovation platforms for selected horticultural crops such as tomato, African bush mango, and pineapple. Innovation platforms are an avenue to bring together stakeholders having a common interest in identifying and solving problems in a particular value chain. Dr. Amao has also been involved in technology and knowledge transfer in various aspects of horticulture. Her research interests include socio-economic studies in horticultural value chains and development economics.

Dr. Iyabo Bosede Adeoye is Assistant Director of Research at the National Horticultural Research Institute, Ibadan, Nigeria. She obtained her Ph.D. in Agricultural Economics from the University of Ibadan, Nigeria. She specializes in value chain development, production, post-harvest economics, market intelligence, analysis of horticultural crops, and monitoring and evaluation of agricultural projects. Gender dimensions and women empowerment along the horticultural value chain also form part of her roles and responsibilities. Dr. Adeoye is a fellow of African Women in Agricultural Research and Development (AWARD 2013). She participated in the Australia Africa Award “Increasing Development Impact of Agricultural Research” (2018), Netherlands Fellowship Programmes on Market Access for Sustainable Development (2011), Managing for Sustainable Impact (2019), and Horticultural Sector Development for Emerging Markets (2021).

# Contents

# Preface

This book, *Agricultural Economics*, discusses pertinent aspects of agricultural economics and rural development. It is divided into three sections. The first section consists of four chapters that examine case studies of agricultural/rural development-related projects and activities. Chapter 1 examines the impact of off-season summer tomato cultivation on the income and food security of growers. The study reveals a positive impact of off-season tomato cultivation on growers' income. Consumption expenditure and food security status of tomato growers are also observed to increase significantly in comparison to non-growers. Chapter 2 discusses the effect of the Agropolitan project in Malaysia on rural development and poverty eradication. The study finds that the Agropolitan project led to a significant increase in income and a move out of poverty for participants. Chapter 3 discusses government activities on social protection and safety nets in Bangladesh. Chapter 4 uses a qualitative content approach to examine the value chain of brandy production. This study finds that contract farming is beneficial to both processing companies and smallholder farmers. The second section reviews factors affecting the efficiency of vegetable production and the basics of good business plans for small-scale agribusiness investors in Nigeria. Chapter 5 looks at three frontline crops in Nigeria: tomato, pepper, and onion. The study recommends that increased awareness of stakeholders on optimum levels of resource use is germane to increasing agricultural productivity of these vegetables. Chapter 6 provides a synthesis of planning small-scale entrepreneurial skills to guide the current and prospective micro investors to harness wide ranges of agribusiness value chains in Nigeria. The third and final section includes Chapter 7, which deals with farmers' knowledge of a novel method of livestock production called organic livestock farming. The chapter highlights the need to improve farmers' knowledge of this novel method through the strengthening of an extension service system.

**Dr. Ifeoluwapo O. Amao and Dr. Iyabo B. Adeoye**
National Horticultural Research Institute,
Ibadan, Nigeria

# Section 1

# Case Studies

Chapter 1

# Impact of Off-Season Summer Tomato Cultivation on Income and Food Security of the Growers

*Md. Sadique Rahman and Debasish Chandra Acharjee*

## Abstract

Vegetable production can help farmers to generate income, which will eventually alleviate poverty and malnutrition. Tomato is one of the most important vegetables in Bangladesh. But tomato production is extremely sensitive to hot and wet growing conditions. Thus, few varieties of off-season summer tomato have been developed and disseminated. Keeping these factors in consideration, this chapter was designed to delineate the impacts of summer tomato adoption on the income and food security status of the growers in a region of Bangladesh. Findings indicated that off-season tomato growers received significantly higher income. Consumption expenditure and food security status of the off-season tomato growers were significantly higher than non-growers. The chapter also includes policy implications for further development of the technology.

**Keywords:** Bangladesh, food consumption score, off-season, summer tomato, well-being

## 1. Introduction

Bangladesh's agriculture contributed around 16% of the country's GDP and currently employs around 45% of the country's labor force [1]. Crop sector in Bangladesh is characterized by rice monoculture, which has led to a number of serious physical and biological problems, including nutritional impact [2]. However, recently, emphasis is also shifting from basic nutrients to balanced diets. Vegetables can play an important role by providing high nutritive value food and higher returns that eventually alleviate poverty. Due to favorable climatic and soil, a large number of vegetables are cultivated throughout the year in Bangladesh. In a view of increase in income, employment, and reduction of widespread malnutrition in Bangladesh, there is a strong need for vegetable cultivation.

Among the vegetables, tomato is one of the most important vegetables by acreage, production, yield, commercial use, and consumption. Tomato is cultivated all over the country due to its adaptability to wide range of soil and climate [3]. Its demand for both domestic and foreign markets has increased manifold due to its excellent nutritional and processing qualities [4]. In Bangladesh, congenial atmosphere remains for tomato production during low temperature winter season, that is, early November is the best time for tomato planting in Bangladesh [5]. Tomato plants are highly sensitive to hot and humid seasons. However, limited attempt has been made to overcome this high temperature barrier.

Considering the growing demand and importance of tomato, Bangladesh Agricultural Research Institute (BARI) has developed and disseminated few varieties of off-season summer tomatoes. This summer season tomato cultivation requires complex agronomic management including high labor and applications of growth regulators in addition to extended skill and knowledge. Farmers typically plant off-season tomato varieties in the middle of May and continued cultivation up to February in the following year. To protect tomato plants from monsoon rain, farmers construct a bamboo pole frame and slats to which a polyethylene hoop-shaped roof is attached [6]. The farm-level adoption of these varieties has already created a wide range of socioeconomic impacts that need to be evaluated properly to understand the output of research and development. So far, very little information is available on the impact of off-season tomato cultivation in Bangladesh.

Cultivating summer tomatoes in Bangladesh holds promise as a profitable enterprise with which farmers can augment the existing cropping patterns since only small amounts of land are required [6–8]. A study was conducted in southwestern Bangladesh to quantify the effect of training farmers on off-season vegetable cultivation. Findings indicate that training increased the net household income by about 48%. There was a significant increase in pesticide use and although there was an improvement in pesticide-handling practices, trained farmers may have been more exposed to pesticide health risk [9]. Majority of the off-season tomato growers possessed high knowledge on summer tomato cultivation. Education, land possession, annual family income, and extension contact of the farmers had a positive significant relationship with the farmers' knowledge on summer tomato cultivation [10]. Attack by pest and disease, lack of seed at proper time, lack of agricultural credit, and high cost of production were the major constraints for the adoption of summer tomato.

From the above discussion, it is clear that impacts of off-season tomato cultivation have not been addressed well in Bangladesh. Studies only measure the profitability using a very small number of samples. Thus, the questions like "What is the impact of off-season tomato cultivation on income and food security status?" are yet to be studied empirically in Bangladesh. This chapter is a moderate effort to examine the above research question and fulfill the gaps to some extent. It is expected that the findings will help the scientists and policy makers to further develop the technology.

## 2. Production technology of off-season tomato

Summer tomato cultivation in Bangladesh is mainly constrained by the seasonality and frequent attack of diseases. During the summer, fruit settings were disrupted due to high daytime temperatures above 26°C and at night temperatures above 20°C [11]. To overcome this problem, Bangladesh Agricultural Research Institute (BARI) has developed few hybrid varieties of heat tolerant tomato, known as off-season summer tomato [6]. High to medium land is required for summer tomato cultivation. Tomato may be grown on a wide range of soil from sandy to clay. The raised bed planting can be adopted in low land tropics and high rainfall areas. Transparent poly tunnel with a height of 120-180 cm was built on the raised beds to protect the tomato plants from rain. Approximately 75 cm wide drainage channel need must be constructed between tunnels to facilitate irrigation, drainage, and other intercultural operations [6].

## 3. Data sources and analytical techniques

The present study mainly used primary data to achieve the objectives. The primary data was collected from Jashore region (**Figure 1**) of Bangladesh due to the higher concentration of off-season summer tomato cultivation [6, 8]. At first, summer tomato cultivating villages was selected and for those villages a complete list of the off-season summer tomato growers was prepared taking help from local agricultural extension office. From that list, a total of 100 farmers were selected randomly as growers of summer tomato to collect the information regarding off-season tomato cultivation. These farmers were trained by different organizations on management aspect of summer tomato cultivation. Besides 150 farmers who

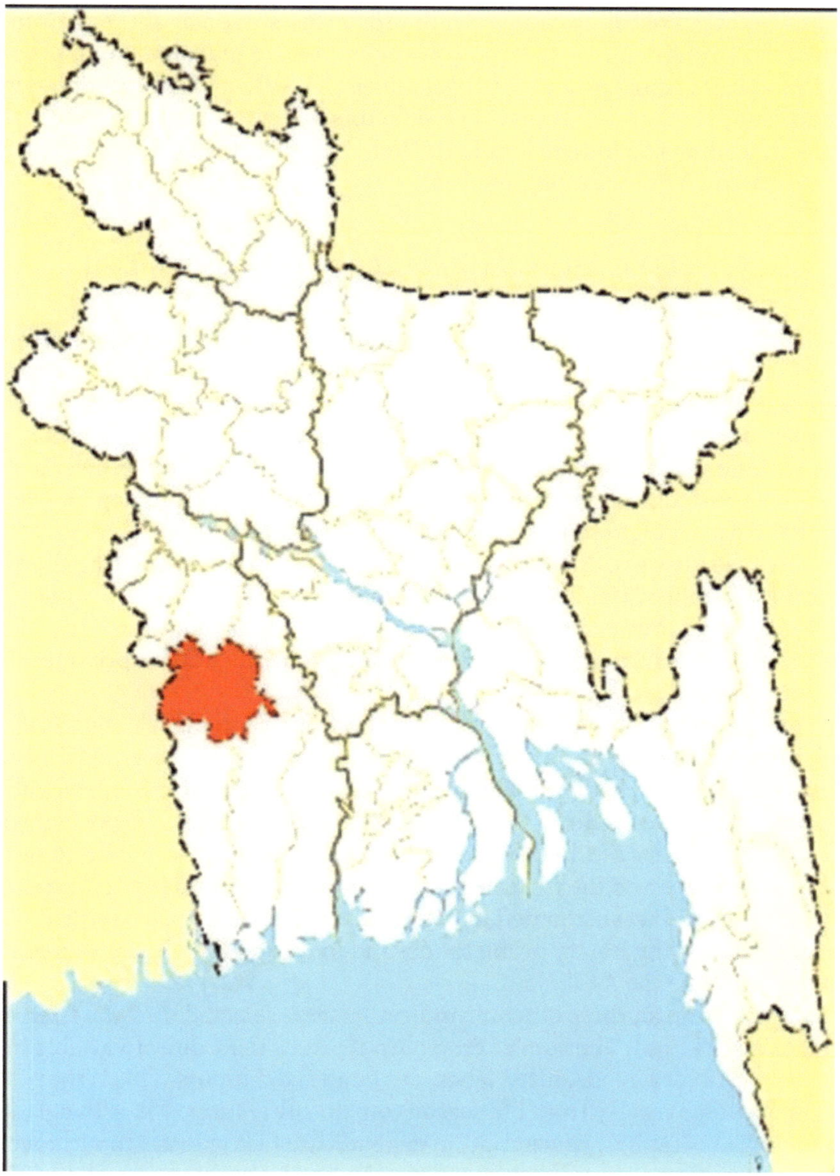

**Figure 1.**
*Location map.*

did not cultivate off-season summer tomato but had suitable land and interest in growing summer tomato were selected randomly for interview as non-growers of the technology. The non-growers grew winter tomato and also did not receive any training on summer tomato cultivation. Thus, a total of 250 farmers were selected randomly for the face-to-face interview.

The present study employed propensity score matching (PSM), inverse probability weighting (IPW), and inverse probability weighted regression adjustment (IPWRA) techniques to achieve the objectives. PSM constructs a statistical comparison group that is based on a model of the probability of participating in the treatment, using observed characteristics [12]. According to Heckman et al. [13], the basic assumption of using a counterfactual is that the untreated samples approximate the treated sample if they had not been treated, that is, E ($Y_{0i}$ T = 1). The validity of PSM depends on two condition; conditional independence assumption (CIA) and sizable common support in propensity score across the growers and non-growers. The CIA argues that program outcomes are independent of program participation conditional on a set of observables (X). When CIA condition is not met, it is assumed that may be unobserved factors affect the outcome and treatment assignment, leading to a hidden bias [14]. Under the CIA, the average treatment effect on treated (ATT) was computed as:

$$ATT = E(Y1 - Y0 \mid X, T=1) = E(Y1 \mid X, T=1) - E(Y0 \mid X, T=0) \quad (1)$$

Balancing properties need to be satisfied for PSM to be valid which implies that for observation with the same propensity score, the distribution of pretreatment characteristics must be same across growers and non-growers' group. Another requirement for PSM is common support or overlap condition. It implies that farmers with same X values have positive probability of being both grower and non-grower. Three matching algorithms: nearest neighbor, radius matching and kernel matching were used to present the findings of the study.

IPW uses the inverse of the propensity score as weights in calculating the average value of the outcome variable [15, 16]. IPW does not match off-season tomato growers with non-growers. In IPW, farmers with low predicted probability receive a lower weight while farmers with high predicted probability of adoption receive a higher weight.

True measurement of impacts requires controlling of sample selection bias through random assignment of individuals into treatments. However, ATT from PSM and IPW can still produce biased results in the presence of mis-specification in the propensity score model [17, 18]. To overcome the problem, the present study used IPWRA which has the double-robust property that ensures consistent results as it allows the outcome and the treatment model to account for mis-specification. ATT in the IPWRA model was estimated in two steps. In the first step, we estimated the propensity scores using binary probit model and in second step, linear regression was used to estimate the ATT.

To assess the impact three outcome indicators were selected. Income from off-season tomato (Tk./ha): The sum of crop output minus the value of variable inputs (fertilizers, pesticides, seeds, hired labor, etc.) and fixed inputs. This is the net income households receive from off-season tomato cultivation (Tk. is Bangladeshi currency, 1 USD = Tk. 85). Consumption expenditure (Tk./adult): Total expenditure on consumption per adult per year was calculated. Food security status: Food security status of the farmers was assessed by using Food Consumption Score (FCS). The FCS of a household is calculated by multiplying the frequency of foods consumed in the last seven days with the weighting of each food group [19].

## 4. Profitability of off-season tomato cultivation

It is conspicuous from **Figure 2** that the average yield of summer tomato was 32.45 t/ha which was significantly higher than that of the winter tomato growers. In the winter season, farmers usually received Tk 10 as selling price of per kg tomato, while in the case of summer tomato farmers they received Tk. 38 per kg, which is substantially high. Due to higher productivity and price, the gross return for off-season tomato growers was also significantly higher. Higher gross return implies higher profit. Thus, off-season tomato cultivation may reduce poverty to some extent. **Figure 3** indicates that off-season tomato cultivation does not have any cost advantage. **Figure 4** indicates that tunnel preparation cost, human labor cost, and growth regulators were the major cost items for off-season tomato cultivation [6, 7]. It implies that off-season tomato cultivation is cost incentive and requires higher initial investment which confirms the findings of other studies [20, 21].

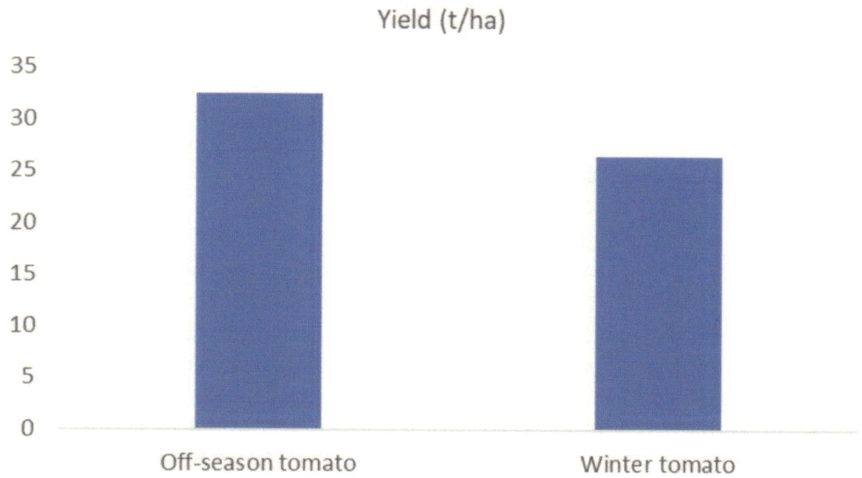


**Figure 2.**
*Comparative yield of tomato.*

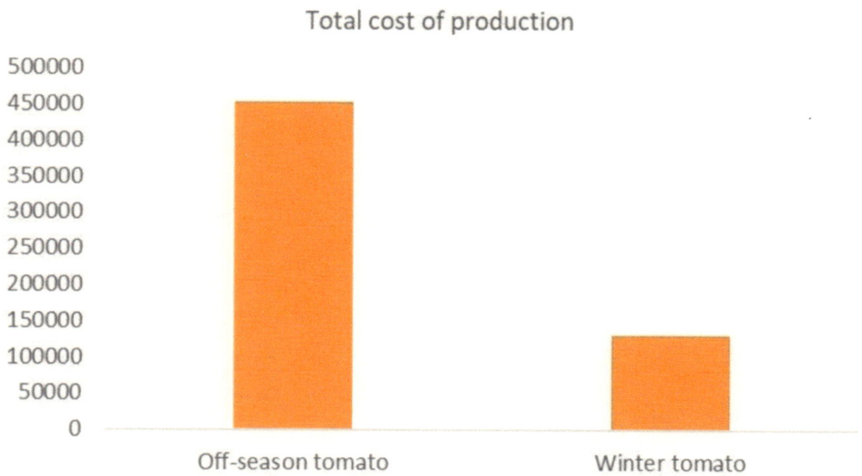


**Figure 3.**
*Comparative cost of production.*

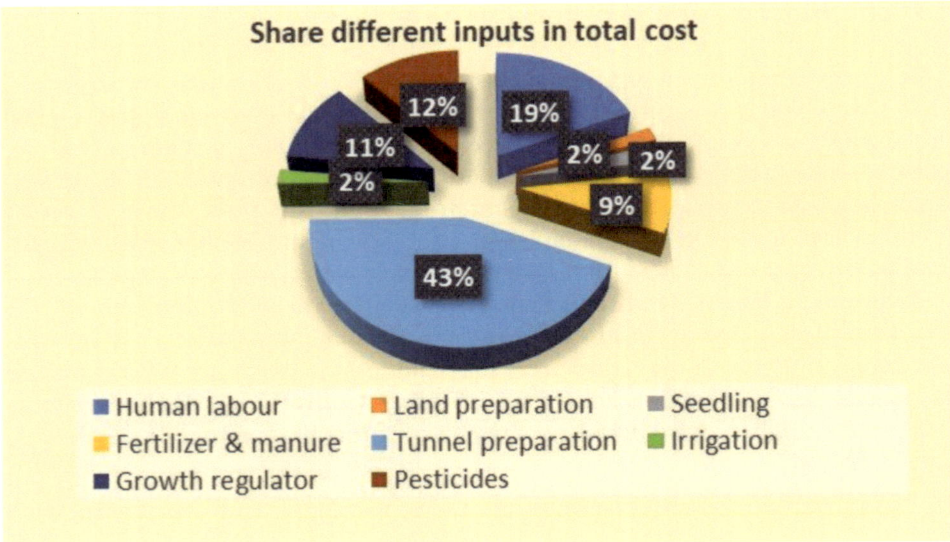


**Figure 4.**
*Share of different inputs.*

## 5. Impacts of off-season tomato cultivation

The off-season tomato growers received significantly higher income compared to non-growers (winter season growers) based on nearest neighbor, radius, and kernel matching (**Table 1**). This may be due to higher productivity and market price. Ali et al. [20] also indicated that off-season tomato cultivation is profitable. The ATT values were found to be Tk. 261,000, 253,000, and 261,000 based on nearest neighbor, radius, and kernel matching, respectively. The findings of IPW and IPWRA were similar to PSM which confirms the robustness of the results. The ATT values were Tk. 257,667, and 257,683 based on IPW and IPWRA, respectively. The income from off-season tomato cultivation can be further increased by improving management practices, such as timing of various growth regulators application [6, 22]. Thus, there is scope to raise the income reducing costs by appropriate management practice. The studies suggested that training on off-season tomato cultivation has significant impact of income [9]. Therefore, more efforts on trained farmers may also provide better results.

| Models | ATT | SE | t-Value |
|---|---|---|---|
| PSM | | | |
| NN matching | 261,000*** | 20,427 | 12.78 |
| Kernel matching | 253,000*** | 21,713 | 11.65 |
| Radius matching | 261,000*** | 18,406 | 14.19 |
| IPW | 257,667*** | 19,915 | 12.94 |
| IPWRA | 257,683*** | 20,101 | 12.82 |

****Indicates significant at 1% level.*
*Nearest neighbor, kernel matching, and radius matching identified 34, 98, and 98 farmers as non-growers (control), respectively.*

**Table 1.**
*Impact of off-season tomato cultivation on income.*

| Models | ATT | SE | t-Value |
|---|---|---|---|
| PSM | | | |
| NN matching | 10,183*** | 2520 | 4.04 |
| Kernel matching | 9346*** | 1491 | 6.26 |
| Radius matching | 7584*** | 1228 | 6.17 |
| IPW | 8545*** | 1410 | 6.06 |
| IPWRA | 8449*** | 1425 | 5.93 |

****Indicates significant at 1% level.*

**Table 2.**
*Impact of off-season tomato cultivation on consumption expenditure.*

| Models | ATT | SE | t-Value |
|---|---|---|---|
| PSM | | | |
| NN matching | 7.09* | 4.47 | 1.59 |
| Kernel matching | 4.04 | 2.75 | 1.47 |
| Radius matching | 5.87*** | 1.85 | 3.16 |
| IPW | 4.63** | 2.12 | 2.18 |
| IPWRA | 4.43** | 2.17 | 2.03 |

**, ** and *** indicates significant at 10%, 5%, and 1% level, respectively*

**Table 3.**
*Impact of off-season tomato cultivation on FCS.*

The consumption expenditure per adult is also significantly higher for off-season tomato growers compared to non-growers based on nearest neighbor, radius, and kernel matching (**Table 2**). The findings of IPW and IPWRA were also similar to PSM which confirms the robustness of the results. The ATT values were found to be Tk. 8545 and 8449 based on IPW and IPWRA, respectively. Due to higher income off-season tomato growers were able to spend more on consumption. Karim et al. [7] also indicated that off-season tomato growers were able to increase their socioeconomic status due to higher income.

FCS was used as proxy to capture the impact of off-season tomato cultivation on food security of the growers. The findings of PSM analysis indicate that off-season tomato cultivation has significant effect on the FCS of the growers. FCS was significantly higher for off-season tomato growers compared to non-growers based on nearest neighbor, and radius matching (**Table 3**). The ATT values were 7.09 and 5.87 based on nearest neighbor and radius matching, respectively. The ATT values were also significant at the 5% level for the other two methods which confirm the robustness of the findings. Off-season tomato cultivation can be a useful way of increasing the income and food security status of the farmers. More awareness building programs and extension efforts are warranted to increase the area under off-season tomato cultivation.

## 6. Constraints of off-season tomato cultivation

Although off-season tomato cultivation is observed to be a profitable crop, but there are several constraints to its higher production. Eighty percent of the farmers reported frequent attack of insect and diseases was the major constraint that hinders the adoption and production confirm the findings of Ali et al. [20] (**Table 4**).

| Items | Percent | Rank |
|---|---|---|
| Attack of insect and diseases | 80 | 1 |
| High price of growth hormone | 75 | 2 |
| High price of tunnel materials | 60 | 3 |

**Table 4.**
*Constraints of off-season tomato cultivation.*

High price of tunnel materials and growth hormone require high cash amount for cultivation which in turns hinder the adoption process and production. More research on off-season tomato varieties is essential to optimize the technology.

## 7. Conclusions

It is evident that off-season tomato cultivation is profitable and has significant impact on the consumption expenditure and food security status of the farmers. Based on the results, a number of policy implications can be drawn. More investment in research and development is needed from both donor and government agencies to develop resistant varieties of off-season tomato since the farmers reported that frequent attack of insects and diseases was the main constraint of off-season tomato cultivation. Efforts are needed to disseminate the off-season tomato cultivation technique to different parts of the country. Cost of production is higher for off-season tomato cultivation compared to winter season tomato cultivation. Steps to diversify sources of income as well as access to low interest credit can increase the availability of capital. Higher income may have a positive effect on reducing poverty in the country. Higher consumption expenditure and food security status may play a vital role in reducing malnutrition. Thus, there is a need for promoting the role of off-season tomato cultivation in anti-poverty programs, especially in developing countries like Bangladesh.

## Acknowledgements

The authors are grateful to farmers and the enumerators for their cooperation during data collection. The authors are grateful to the Social Science Research Council, Planning Division, Ministry of Planning, People's Republic of Bangladesh for financial support to conduct the study.

## Conflict of interest

The authors declare no conflict of interest.

**Author details**

Md. Sadique Rahman[1]* and Debasish Chandra Acharjee[2]

1 Department of Management and Finance, Sher-e-Bangla Agricultural University, Dhaka, Bangladesh

2 Department of Agribusiness, Bangabandhu Sheikh Mujibur Rahman Agricultural University, Gazipur, Bangladesh

*Address all correspondence to: saadrhmn@yahoo.com

## References

[1] BBS. Yearbook of Agricultural Statistics of Bangladesh. Dhaka: Bangladesh Bureau of Statistics, Statistical Division, Ministry of Planning, Government of the People's Republic of Bangladesh; 2015

[2] Saha N. An economic analysis of homestead vegetables production in some selected areas of Netrokona district [MS thesis]. Mymensingh, Bangladesh: Department of Agricultural Economics, Bangladesh Agricultural University; 2012

[3] Ahmed KU. Phul Phal O Shak Shabji (in Bangla). 2nd ed. Dhaka, Bangladesh: Farm Gate; 1976. p. 470

[4] Hossain MA, Goffer MA, Chowdhury JCS, Rahman MS, Hossain MI. A study on postharvest practices and loss of tomato in some selected areas of Bangladesh. Bangladesh Journal of Agricultural Research. 1999;**24**(2):299

[5] Hossain MM, Karim MK, Haque MM, Hassain AKMA. Performance of Some Promising Tomato Lines Planted at Different Dates. Gazipur: Annual Report, Vegetable Section, Division of Horticulture, Bangladesh Agricultural Research Institute; 1986. pp. 9-12

[6] Baksh ME, Rossi F, Krupnik TJ, Talukder ASMH, McDonald A. How much can smallholders in Bangladesh benefit from summer tomato cultivation? An applied agro-economic analysis of on-farm data. SAARC Journal of Agriculture. 2015;**13**:80-93 https://doi.org/10.3329/sja.v13i2.26570

[7] Karim MR, Rahman MS, Alam MS. Profitability of summer BARI hybrid tomato cultivation in Jessore district of Bangladesh. Journal of Agriculture and Rural Development. 2009;**7**(1&2):73-79. DOI: 10.3329/jard.v7i1.4424

[8] Hajong P, Sikder B, Mondal S, Islam MA. Adoption and profitability of summer tomato cultivation in Jashore district of Bangladesh. Bangladesh Journal of Agricultural Research. 2018;**43**(4):575-585. DOI: 10.3329/bjar.v43i4.39154

[9] Schreinemachers P, Wu M, Uddin MN, Ahmed S, Hanson P. Farmers training in off-season vegetables: Effects on income and pesticide use in Bangladesh. Food Policy. 2016;**61**:132-140. DOI: 10.1016/j.foodpol. 2016.03.002

[10] Monalesa N. Farmers' knowledge and attitude towards summer tomato cultivation [MS thesis]. Dhaka, Bangladesh: Department of Agricultural Extension and Information System, Sher-e-Bangla Agricultural University; 2014

[11] Zaman MM, Huq SMA, Chowdhury MJA. Production potentiality of summer tomato in Jamalpur region. International Journal of Sustainable Crop Production. 2006;**1**(2):12-15

[12] Khandker SR, Koolwar GB, Samad HA. Handbook of Impact Evaluation; Quantitative Methods and Practice. Washington DC: The World Bank; 2010

[13] Heckman JJ, Ichimura H, Todd P. Matching as an econometric evaluation estimator. Review of Economic Studies. 1998;**65**:261-294

[14] Caliendo M, Kopeinig S. Some practical guidance for the implementation of propensity score matching. Journal of Economic Surveys. 2008;**22**(1):31-72. DOI: 10.1111/j.1467-6419.2007.00527.x

[15] Wooldridge JM. Inverse probability weighted estimation for general missing

data problems. Journal of Econometrics. 2007;**141**:1281-1301. DOI: 10.1016/j.jeconom.2007.02.002

[16] Imbens G. Nonparametric estimation of average treatment effects under exogeneity: A review. Review of Economics and Statistics. 2004;**86**(1):4-29. DOI: 10.1162/003465304323023651

[17] Robins J, Sued M, Lei-Gomez Q, Rotnitzky A. Comment: Performance of double-robust estimators when "inverse probability" weights are highly variable. Statistical Science. 2007;**22**(4):544-559. DOI: 10.1214/07-STS227D

[18] Wooldridge JM. Econometric Analysis of Cross Section and Panel Data. 2nd ed. London, England: The MIT Press; 2010

[19] WFP. Food Consumption Analysis Calculation and Use of the Food Consumption Score in Food Security Analysis. Rome: World Food Programme, Vulnerability Analysis and Mapping Branch; 2008. Available from: https://www.wfp.org/content/technical-guidance-sheet-food-consumption-analysis-calculation-and-use-food-consumption-score-food-s

[20] Ali Q, Ashfaq M, Khan MTI. An economic analysis of off-season tomato production in Punjab. The Journal of Animal & Plant Sciences. 2017;**27**(1):294-301

[21] Adenuga AH, Lawal AM, Rotimi OA. Economics and technical efficiency of dry season tomato production in selected areas in Kwara State, Nigeria. Agris On-Line Papers in Economics and Informatics. 2013;**5**:11-19

[22] Chen JT, Hanson P. Summer Tomato Production Using Fruit-Setting Hormones. AVRDC Publication No. 01-511. Taiwan: Asian Vegetable Research and Development Centre (AVRDC); 2001

Chapter 2

# Agropolitan Project: Role in Rural Development and Poverty Eradication

*Mohd Khairi Ismail, Chamhuri Siwar and Muhamad Zahid Muhamad*


## Abstract

Theoretical discussions on vicious cycle of poverty shows poverty is a societal problem involving various factors and difficult to overcome. Hence, the efforts to resolve it are necessary as it gives negative impression to society and country. In Malaysia, poverty rate in rural areas remain higher than in urban areas. The situation has prompted the government to focus its efforts to eradicate poverty in the rural area. The Agropolitan project is an incentive by Malaysian government, introduced in 2007 to eradicate poverty in rural areas by increasing the income of participants. This chapter will consider the Agropolitan Project of Gahai, Malaysia as a case study. Discussion of the case study for Agropolitan Gahai Project has shown how its implementation can contribute to the alleviation through increasing income of participants whereby participants were not categorized poor and helped them move out of the vicious cycle of poverty.


**Keywords:** Agropolitan, rural development, poverty eradication

## 1. Introduction

Poverty is an issue that is still a concern in most countries of the world. It is a complex phenomenon and covers many dimensions and is closely related to human and social behavior [1]. It is estimated that over 1.2 billion people around the world are in a state of poverty in which 26% are categorized as low national income, 58% with moderate national income, and 17% as medium high national income [2]. Poverty in many countries also tends to be concentrated in rural areas than in the city. According to [3], more than three quarters of poor society members are those who live in rural areas. The poor are expected to continue to live in rural areas for several decades. The issue of poverty is giving a signal to all parties to continue efforts to eradicate poverty.

Globally, aggressive efforts to eradicate poverty can be viewed through the implementation of the Millennium Development Goals (MDGs) which involves 15 years of duration since year 2000. The implementation of the MDGs are aimed at eradicating poverty, aimed at eight goals, namely eradicating extreme poverty and hunger; achieving universal basic education; achieving gender equality and empower women; reducing the rate of children's mortality; improving the health state of mothers; preventing human immunodeficiency virus (HIV)/acquired immunodeficiency syndrome (AIDS), malaria, and other diseases; ensuring the preservation and sustainability of nature; and promoting global cooperation. Report of [4] showed greater success in eradicating poverty in the last 15 years. According to the report:

i. Since 1990, the number of people who live in the conditions of extreme poor has been reduced by 50% worldwide.

ii. The proportion of individuals who do not have sufficient nutrients has been reduced by almost 50% worldwide.

iii. School admission rates in the developing region has reached 91% and increasing number of female students compared to 15 years ago.

iv. Promising efforts against HIV/AIDS, malaria, and tuberculosis.

v. The rate of deaths of children under 5 years old has been reduced more than half, and the death of mothers has declined by 45% in the whole world.

Presently, efforts to eradicate poverty continued through the implementation of Sustainable Development Goals (SDG). SDG has established the eradication of all forms of poverty in the society. In the year 2030, all individuals are targeted to not suffer any form of poverty where people strive to live with a minimum of USD$1.25 per day. In addition to that, some of the goals were also determined, that is:

i. Eradicate extreme poverty for all people everywhere

ii. Reduce at least by half the proportion of men, women, and children of all ages living in poverty according to the dimensions determined by respective nation

iii. Implement nationally appropriate social protection systems and measures for all, including the poor, and by 2030 achieve substantial coverage of the poor and the vulnerable

iv. Ensure that the poor and vulnerable have equal access to economic resources, as well as access to basic services, ownership, and control over land and other ownership.

v. Building the resilience of the poor toward vulnerability.

vi. Implementation of policies and programs that can eliminate multi-dimensional poverty.

vii. Establish a strong framework at national, regional, and international level that addresses development strategies for poverty alleviation.

In the Malaysian context, the reduction of poverty rates is strongly contributed by the policy implementation by the government, through four major policies, namely New Economic Policy (NEP) (1970–1990), the National Development Policy (NDP) (1990–2000), National Vision Policy (NVP) (2001–2010), New Economic Model (MBE) (2010), and Shared Prosperity Vision (SPV 2030). Malaysia has managed to reduce the rate of poverty from 49.3% in the year 1970 to 0.4% in the year 2016 as in **Table 1**.

The national poverty rate in Malaysia has declined from 49.3% in the year 1970 to 0.6% the year 2014. Poverty analysis based on strata showed declining trend in the urban and rural areas. In the urban area, the rate continued to decline to 0.3 % in the year 2014 compared to 21.3% in 1970. The rural area exhibited the same declining trend from the year 1970 until the year 2014, but with a slight rise in 2009. Despite the decreasing trend in both areas, during the years from 1970 to 2017, the rate of poverty in rural areas remained higher than in the urban. The difference in the rate of poverty is pushing the government to focus its efforts to eradicate poverty in the rural areas.

| Year | Percentage (%) | | |
|---|---|---|---|
| | Malaysia | Urban | Rural |
| 1970 | 49.3 | 21.3 | 58.7 |
| 1976 | 37.7 | 15.4 | 45.7 |
| 1979 | 37.4 | 17.5 | 45.8 |
| 1984 | 20.7 | 8.5 | 27.3 |
| 1987 | 19.4 | 8.5 | 24.8 |
| 1989 | 16.5 | 7.1 | 21.1 |
| 1992 | 12.4 | 4.7 | 21.2 |
| 1995 | 8.7 | 3.6 | 14.9 |
| 1997 | 6.1 | 2.1 | 10.9 |
| 1999 | 8.5 | 3.3 | 14.8 |
| 2002 | 6.0 | 2.3 | 13.5 |
| 2004 | 5.7 | 2.5 | 11.9 |
| 2007 | 3.6 | 2.0 | 7.1 |
| 2009 | 3.8 | 1.7 | 8.4 |
| 2012 | 1.7 | 1.0 | 3.4 |
| 2014 | 0.6 | 0.3 | 1.6 |
| 2016 | 0.4 | 0.2 | 1.0 |

*Source: [5–7].*

**Table 1.**
*Poverty incidents in Malaysia 1970–2016.*

Rural poverty eradication has been government's priority because there are more than 36% of Malaysia's population (10.34 million people population) living in rural areas [7]. Therefore, the efforts to eradicate rural poverty and develop the rural areas have been given priority by the government. Among the policies and programs that have been implemented are Rural Development Master Plan (PIPLB), Indigenous Development Strategic Planning, Rural Mega Uplifting Program (PLMLB), New Model for Rural Economy (MBELB), Rural Transformation Centers (RTC) and Government Transformation Program that involve Sustainable Village Program. Rural Development and Master Plan (PIPLB), Strategic Development Plan for Indigenous People, Mega Rural Uplift Program (PLMLB), New Rural Economy Model (MBELB), and National and Rural Transformation Programs.

Among the programs to eradicate extreme poverty was implemented through the Rural Mega Uplifting Program (PLMLB) is Agropolitan project. Since 2006 till 2007, a total of 44,000 people from extreme poverty have been identified in Malaysia. Four ministries, inclusive of the Ministry of Agriculture, the Ministry of Women, Family and Community Development and Ministry of Rural and Regional Development (MRRD) were responsible for eradicating poverty which involves 10,000 people from extreme poverty cluster. At the same time, the government established five development corridors namely the Northern Corridor Economic Region (NCER), East Coast Economic Region (ECER), Sabah Development Corridor (SDC), Sarawak Renewable Energy Corridor (SCORE), and Iskandar Malaysia (ISKANDAR). Through the implementation of the five corridors, 4400 individuals from extreme poverty were placed under the implementing agencies of the respective corridors. The remaining 5600 individuals coming from extreme poverty group were handed over to MRRD for poverty eradication planning and become a focus for participating in the Agropolitan program [8].

As of 2017, there were 11 projects under agropolitan programs which have been implemented and involved five states under the supervision of the Ministry of Rural Development Affairs and Regional Development (MRRD) [9]. According to the ministry, there are two successful agropolitan programs which are Gahai Agropolitan Programme, Lipis, Pahang and Batang Lupar Agropolitan Program, Sarawak. Based on the poverty index, namely Poverty Lines Income (PLI), all participants for both agropolitan programs have been classified as non-poor after joining the agropolitan programs which were implemented since 2007 [10].

## 2. Vicious cycle poverty theory and agropolitan mechanism

Poverty is a system that associates certain factors and affects each other. This concept corresponds to poverty factors and turned to beginning points of the poverty vicious cycle and ultimately prevents the development process [11]. With regards to poverty, rural sectors and farming activities participation is considered as a trap of poverty for individuals. Individuals in the rural areas are engaged in low scale production activities that affected their income. This situation is described as a setback and as a barrier and a system which connects barriers and causing the poor to fall into vicious cycle. If left unattended continuously, this will cause the poor will not be able to get food, health, and education adequately. In addition, poverty will cause the poor to not being able change or raise the standard of living better than their parents. The situation is due to low income and poverty that is sustained from generation to another generation as depicted in **Figure 1** that shows the poverty vicious cycle. At individual level, vicious cycle could be initiated by the poverty faced caused by failure to meet the nutritional diet requirement. Less nutritious diet intake ultimately affects health and the ability to work. Due to health issues, individuals are not able to work efficiently, and this leads to low productivity. The situation affects their ability to raise their income and thus continue to be in a state of poverty.

Poverty faced by individuals will also affect members of the family. Due to poverty, people are not able to provide sufficient and nutritious food to members of the family, particularly children, and will inhibit their mental growth. The study [12] found the lack of nutritious food affects children's health and eventually

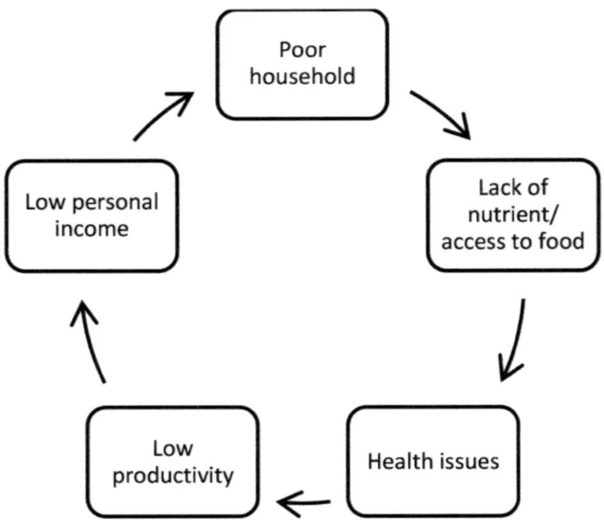


**Figure 1.**
*Individual poverty vicious cycle. Source: [12].*

will contribute to weakening education and contribute to the low education achievement. Failure to obtain education causes them to continue to be engaged in low-income activities and consequently remain to be in a poor situation.

Even though the Vicious Cycle Theory can explain the poverty faced by individuals is associated with poverty factors, there was some criticism of the theory. First, this theory does not explain in detail the concept of poverty and setback. Secondly, the theory does not consider the differences of poverty faced by every country, and thirdly, the theory discusses poverty in static and unchanged situation. The theory is also unable to give a detailed description on how to overcome the vicious poverty cycle.

Theoretical discussions on vicious poverty cycle shows poverty is a societal problem that involve multiple factors and difficult to overcome. However, attempts to solve it are necessary because failure to alleviate poverty will reflect bad impression on one's society and nation. Gill [13] explained that a country cannot develop because of poverty. Therefore, the efforts to alleviate individuals from poverty should be given attention. According to the Organization for Economic Co-operation and Development (OECD) in [14] explained, there are five factors that allow a person to free oneself from poverty. These involve:

i. Economic ability which refers to the ability of the income, expenditure, and ownership of assets.

ii. People's ability referring to ability to obtain health, education, nutritious food, clean water, and safe place to stay.

iii. Political ability that refers to the ability to get the legislature rights

iv. Socio-cultural ability that refers to individuals' ability to be involved in the community activities.

v. Protection ability that refers to the ability to deal with uncertain situation.

Matin and Hulme [15] discussed the perspective of materialism, which indicates individual is unable to meet the basic requirements due to (i) having low income to expend and (ii) shocks applied that caused the income of individuals to fall under the poverty line. In assisting this group, the government will conduct interventions such as micro-financing programs to increase individual income subsequently overcome poverty. Poverty eradication through this approach is called "poverty reduction" as the first step to increase household income (**Figure 2**).

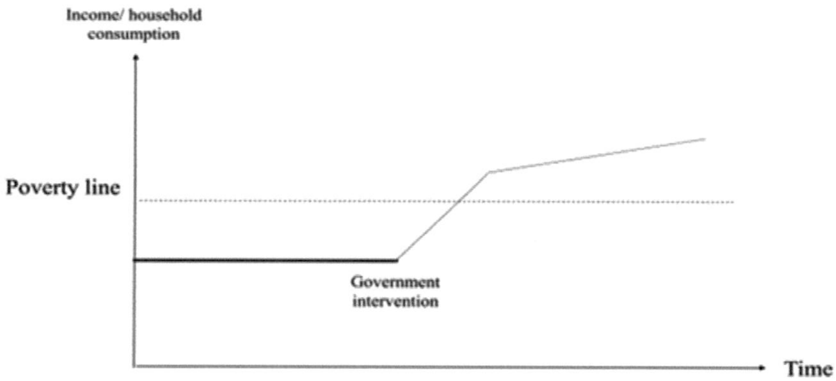


**Figure 2.**
*Reduction of poverty is the first to raise higher revenues contents home. Source: [15].*

In other situation, if shock happens unexpectedly, the situation is just temporary because it only affects the individual's income to obtain food at a certain time. If government intervenes to help people improve their income, this approach refers to the poverty reduction as a "one-off" grant, which would reverse the household income to the previous level (**Figure 3**). Although this approach is simple, it still fails to help the poor. Consequently, there exists the need to promote an approach that emphasizes the multi-dimensional design complex programs (multi-sector and partnerships between organizations), to help the poor. Not only has it met the minimum of physical needs but also access to health, education, and other services.

Sachs [16] in his book "The End of Poverty" discusses that government intervention is important to increase the poor's individual's ability to get the poor out of the situation and able to increase savings and investment which are becoming the driving force to the accumulation of capital to move out of poverty. He said there is a correlation between economic activities, savings, capital investment, and increasing economic activities. Household uses income as a means for consumption, savings, and taxes. The government uses the tax for current spending and development expenses. Capital is generated by household savings and government expenses. Higher capital formation leads to economic growth, which in turn increases household income as a

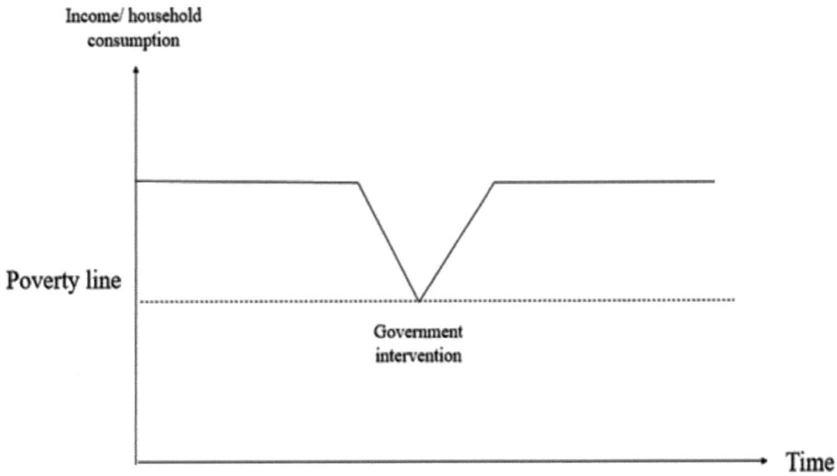


**Figure 3.**
*Poverty reduction as a "one-off" grant that return household income to previous level. Source: [15].*

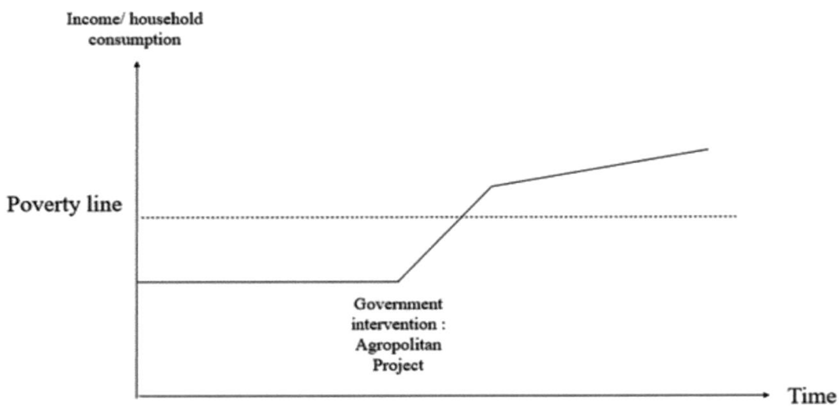


**Figure 4.**
*The Agropolitan project is a government intervention to eradicate poverty to increase income. Source: Adapted from [15].*

result of income growth. Capital assistance for projects would lead to capital accumulation, economic growth, and an income increase among the household members who receive benefits from the given assistance. In the context of this study, Vicious Poverty Cycle Theory describes the poverty situation faced by the extreme poor group. The extreme poor not only lack income but also basic needs such as housing, education, health, and other amenities. This poverty will continue to be inherited by their children to the next generation. The Agropolitan project was a government intervention to eradicate poverty to increase income (**Figure 4**).

## 3. Development of Gahai Agropolitan for rural development and poverty eradication

Agropolitan is a development alternative model which is also known as Region Klauster that was introduced in 1974 by an economist, John Friedman. Agropolitan is a development concept that prioritizes the development of much lower level and aims to improve the socio-economic community in rural area. Agropolitan development highlights network development between urban and rural areas [17–20]. Agropolitan development prioritizes on micro-planning that involves specific target group, government, local research and development (R&D), and education institutions [21]. It is an integrated development involving complete physical and institutional infrastructure as well as optimal resource utilization. Besides, the economic farming and non-farming complement agropolitan development projects as agricultural town. Economic activities in the areas of the Agropolitan project is able to contribute to the region in addition to providing opportunities for employment in off-farm and non-farm and existing commercially available in the agropolitan area. Today, agropolitan has become the choice of several countries in planning rural development by the developing countries such as Indonesia, Nepal, and Malaysia [8, 22, 23].

Agropolitan is different when compared to conventional development models like Growth Pole Model. Conventional development model is "above to below approach" and give priority to competition than cooperation for development [24, 25]. Instead, agropolitan prioritizes planning and cooperation establishment starting from the bottom. **Table 2** shows the agropolitan difference which is also known as Region Klauster and conventional development model namely, Pole Growth Model.

The agropolitan model is also known as the Klauster Regional Model which conducts economic activities that depend on the availability of resources in the development area. The agropolitan concept encouraged the development of side economies in the project area. In terms of urbanization, agropolitan development prioritizes a horizontal (decentralized) urbanization system that has major areas and is linked to the more interior areas. In view of planning, it is decentralized in nature prioritizing on diversifying the economic sectors.

### 3.1 Case study: development of the Agropolitan Gahai Project

The Agropolitan project is one of the government's initiatives to eradicate poverty and also involves several districts in the state of Pahang, Malaysia. According to records, there are 11 agropolitan projects which were launched by the government under the Ministry of Rural and Regional Development (MRRD) until 2016, and Pahang have two agropolitan projects which are the Chemomoi Agropolitan Project and Gahai Agropolitan Project [10]. The implementation of Chemomoi Agropolitan still runs and ends in September 2016. While the process of development of the Gahai Agropolitan Project, Lipis, Pahang has stopped in 2012 and has shown results to participants through the income acquisition.

| Components | Conventional models<br>Growth pole model | Agropolitan model<br>Klauster Region |
|---|---|---|
| Basic sector | Large scale economic activities and management agencies outside economic activities (urban) | Economic activity depends on the availability of resources in the area and encourages the development of side economic activities in key areas. |
| City system | Hierarchy, focused on a number of the population that are associated with the Region Centre Theory | Horizontal, containing the main and rural areas that have specialization and benefits |
| Urban-rural relationship | Spreading the benefits of the urban to the rural area gives trickling effects mutually | Complex urban-rural relationship gives mutual impacts |
| Planning | Based on top to bottom through the planners and implementers | Based on a decentralized system of planning, integration, and coordination of various sectors and activities for urban and rural areas |
| Primary policy | Decentralized industry incentives: industrial estates, transportation, and communications | The variety of activities in agriculture, agro-industry, and manufacturing based on resources, city services, training, and network communication |

*Source: [17].*

**Table 2.**
*Comparison between growth pole model and Agropolitan model.*

The selection of the Gahai Agropolitan Project, Lipis for this study is based on the following criteria:

i. Gahai Agropolitan Project has surpassed the development of more than 5 years and allows the impact study to be conducted.

ii. Gahai Agropolitan Project is in Pahang, which is among the state with highest poverty rate (Malaysia 2015), and it is compatible with the objectives of the study in evaluating the impact of the Agropolitan project in eradicating poverty.

iii. The selection of Gahai Agropolitan Project was proposed from the Ministry of Rural and Regional Development (MRRD) as it is an early established Agropolitan project and has showed good performance and exist necessity in evaluating the project.

Gahai Agropolitan Project, Lipis, Pahang encompasses the area of 238.76 hectares, which involves a total of 80 projects participants. Each participant of the project was selected from the extreme/hardcore poor group. The participants of the project were divided into two categories: 50 individuals with house placements and 30 individuals without placements. Although there are 80 registered participants of the Gahai Agropolitan Project, only 50 local participants are actively involved in economic activities and utilize the benefits of the development of economic components, physical components, and human capital components in the Gahai Agropolitan Project. While another 30% are registered participants but are not involved in economic activities, living in the Gahai Agropolitan Project area and they only receive an annual dividend from the Rubber Industry Smallholders Development Authority (RISDA). Gahai Agropolitan Project, Lipis is managed by the implementing agency, Rubber Industry Smallholders Development Authority (RISDA) which was entrusted by the Ministry of Rural and Regional Development (MRRD). The Gahai Agropolitan Project involves the development of economic, physical, and human capital components.

For the first component, economic activities involving primary and downstream activities contribute to participants' income and thus help to increase the standard of living. Primary economic activities refer to the participation of participants in the Well-Being Farm (Ladang Sejahtera). Presently, 232.69 hectares of Well-Being Farm are planted with 117,940 trees and have been producing incomes in the form of wages and dividends. In addition to that, there are downstream activities that can contribute to the participant's income, majority of them are from the extreme poverty group. This is evidenced by the increase in participants' income. Before joining the Gahai Agropolitan Project, participants who are from the extreme poor were with an average income of RM400 a month. After participating in the Agropolitan project, participants receive income in the form of rubber tapping wage and dividends with an average income of RM1900 per month.

As of May 2015, a total of RM400,000 has been paid to participants as "Well-Being Farm" dividends. For downstream activities, host of bird's nests are still active, which is managed by the Gahai Participants Cooperative (KOPEGA). The project involved initial cost totaling RM58,000 which was contributed by 80 agropolitan participants. The management cost for the project up till May 2015 was RM4,591 which focused on the maintenance and pest control. For bird's nest marketing, it involves the sale of products such as bird's nests and drinks. In 2014, the bird's nest project was already producing output of 8.020 kg with an average price of RM1,200 per kilogram with total income of RM6,000.

Development of physical component also includes home, basic infrastructure, amenities, and business infrastructure. This physical component was provided by the implementing agencies during the project development. Basic infrastructure covering roads in settlements, Rural Water Supply (BALB), Rural Roads (JALB), Village Road Project (PJK), and drain and good drainage system. Besides that, the Gahai Agropolitan Project participants also enjoy the convenience of amenities such as the multi-purpose hall, place of worship, playground, and much more. In addition to the basic physical development, the project development also provided business infrastructure, namely booths, workshops, kiosks, and Small and Medium Enterprises (SMEs) infrastructure.

Besides the economic and physical components development, emphasis is also given to the human capital component. This component refers to the course preparation or training for pre-placement and post-placement. For pre-placement courses, the courses were conducted before participants enter the settlement or participate in agropolitan projects. The course was attended by the head of the households (KIR), and it was for the participants' settlement only. Post-settlement course was conducted continuously after the inclusion of participants in the Agropolitan project. The course is not limited to head of households but also involve members of the house. The courses include on entrepreneurship, skills and technical, spirituality, and family well-being.

### 3.2 Gahai Agropolitan Project participants' profile

The analysis of this study include 50 participants of the Gahai Agropolitan Project who are actively involved in economic activities and utilize the benefits of the development of economic components, physical components, and human capital components in the Gahai Agropolitan Project. A total of 50 participants were defined as the study population. During the survey, only 45 participants of the Gahai Agropolitan Project were actively involved in providing feedback as sampling units. Despite not obtaining the entire project participants, 45 participants were sufficient to be used as a sample using simple random sampling technique. Sampling size is following to [26] if the total population is 50, a total of 44 samples are required, and for this study, it meets the number of samples to be analyzed.

**Table 3** shows the percentage information regarding the profiles of participants of the Gahai Agropolitan Project. Participants' profile shows that the majority of

| n = 45 | | |
|---|---|---|
| **Note** | **Percentage (%)** | **Average** |
| **Gender** | | |
| Male | 82.2 | |
| Female | 17.8 | |
| **Age** | | 46.22 |
| 35 years old and below | 2.2 | |
| 36–40 years old | 22.2 | |
| 41–45 years old | 22.2 | |
| 46–50 years old | 28.9 | |
| 51–55 years old | 11.1 | |
| 56 years old and above | 13.3 | |
| **Education** | | |
| Primary school/UPSR | 26.7 | |
| Secondary school/PMR/SRP | 17.8 | |
| Secondary school/SPM | 51.1 | |
| STPM/certificate | 2.2 | |
| **Main occupation** | | |
| Rubber tapper | 88.9 | |
| Others | 11.1 | |
| **Number of household members** | | 5.60 |
| 1–2 people | 11.1 | |
| 3–4 people | 26.7 | |
| 5–6 people | 44.4 | |
| 7–8 people | 13.3 | |
| More than 9 people | 4.4 | |
| *Source: Gahai Fieldwork, 2017.* | | |

**Table 3.**
*Research respondents.*

respondents (82.2%) are men and the remaining (17.8%) are female. The age breakdown showed participants aged between 46 and 50 years represented the highest (28.9%) followed by the participants aged between 36–40 years and 41–45 years with the same percentage (22.2%). Participants aged 56 years and over also participated but the percentage is small (11.1%). While participants aged 35 years and below are only 2.2% equivalent to one person.

In terms of education, the study shows that the majority of participants, (51.1%) successfully obtained mid-secondary level (Sijil Pelajaran Malaysia [SPM]) while 17.8% graduated with lower secondary (PMR/SRP). About 26.7% of respondents completed with only primary school education up to Primary 6. Even though the number of respondents with primary school education is quite high, most of these respondents are 50 years old and above. Regarding employment, the majority of participants (88.9%) are rubber tappers while the remaining 11.1% are employed in other types of occupation. For respondents who did not rubber tapping as main occupation, they still receive income from the rubber plantation activities which were paid in the form of dividends for their status as project participants. These dividends contribute to their household income.

### 3.3 Agropolitan Projects' role in poverty eradication

The Agropolitan Project's performance evaluation is based on income that is earned by the individual or group of extreme poor who participated in this project. It is compatible with the project's main objectives which is eradicating poverty among the participants through an increase in income. For the case study, the income of participants of the Agropolitan Project was analyzed using descriptive analysis and parametric analysis which is paired sample t-test. Descriptive analysis involves minimum value, maximum value, and participant's average income. Besides that, the paired sample t-test is used to determine whether there is a significant change in participant's income for before and after participating in the Project Agropolitan Gahai, Lipis. Furthermore, income analysis also applied Poverty Line Income (PLI) to determine the number of participants who are categorized as poor. The analysis using PLI provides the latest poverty situation for the Gahai Agropolitan Project participants.

### 3.4 Discrete income analysis

**Table 4** shows the participants monthly income before and after participating in the Gahai Agropolitan Project. The left side of **Table 4** shows the income before participating in the Agropolitan project. The analysis shows the majority of respondents (75.5%) earn income of less than RM1, 000 which is below the poverty line income. There are 17.8% of participants earning incomes of between RM1001 and RM1500 and 4.4% have income of between RM1501 and RM2000. Only 2.2% of participants received income exceeding RM2, 000. The average monthly income of the participants before participating in the Gahai Agropolitan Project is RM920.22. This total income is almost similar to the national PLI.

The right side of **Table 4** also shows the participants income after participating in the Agropolitan Project. The value of the incomes is based on the respondents' feedback on questions related to the monthly average income earned after participating in the project. The income analysis shows all participants of the Agropolitan project obtain incomes exceeding RM 500 a month. There are 8.9% of the participants of the project receiving incomes between RM501 and

| n = 45 | | | |
|---|---|---|---|
| **Before** | | **After** | |
| **Income** | **Percentage (%)** | **Income** | **Percentage (%)** |
| RM500 and below | 11.1 | RM500 and below | 0.0 |
| RM501–RM1000 | 64.4 | RM501–RM1000 | 8.9 |
| RM1001–RM1500 | 17.8 | RM1001–RM1500 | 31.1 |
| RM1501–RM2000 | 4.4 | RM1501–RM2000 | 42.2 |
| RM2000 and above | 2.2 | RM2000 and above | 17.8 |

*Source: Field survey, 2017.*

**Table 4.**
*Participants' income before and after participating in Gahai Agropolitan Project.*

| Paired t-test | | | | |
|---|---|---|---|---|
| Pair differences | | t-value | Degree of freedom (df) | Significance (two sides) |
| Average income | Standard deviation | 8.190 | 44 | 0.000 |
| 718.01111 | 588.08925 | | | |

*Source: Field survey, 2017.*

**Table 5.**
*Participants' income difference before and after joining the Gahai Agropolitan Project.*

| Category | Percentage (%) |
|---|---|
| Poor | 4.4 |
| Not poor | 95.6 |

**Table 6.**
*Gahai Agropolitan Project's participants poverty based on the poverty line income (PLI).*

RM1000. Most of the respondents had income above PLI which is RM850. A total of 91.1% respondents earned incomes above RM1000. Details on the incomes amount show 31.1% of respondents earn incomes RM1001–RM1500, 42.2% earn incomes between RM1501–RM2000, and 17.8% earn more than RM2, 000 and above. Income comparison before and after participating the project shows a significant increment. The average monthly income of the participant after participating in the Gahai Agropolitan Project was RM1628.33. This average income is higher compared to monthly average income prior to joining the Gahai Agropolitan Project.

### 3.5 Income parametric analysis

To further strengthen the analysis, the findings of an increase in a participant's income for involvement in Gahai Agropolitan Project were analyzed using a parametric test, paired sample t-test. The test is carried out using the data of the participants' income before and after participating in the project. **Table 5** shows income differences before and after participating in the Agropolitan project. The analysis show significant differences to the participants' income with a value of $t = 8196$ and the value of $p = 0.000$, indicating that there is a significant income difference before and after participating in the Agropolitan project. Participant's income increased and significant differences were significant before and after participating in the Gahai Agropolitan Project.

### 3.6 Poverty analysis using poverty line income (PLI)

**Table 6** shows the poverty analysis for the Gahai Agropolitan Project's participants using the poverty line income (PLI). Based on the table above, the household is categorized poor should the household receive an income less than the poverty line. This case study applied PLI at a national level in 2014 for Peninsular Malaysia and rural area at RM 840. RM840 value means the households earning incomes less than this value is considered poor. Based on **Table 6**, 95.6% of the Agropolitan project participants are considered not poor, earning income exceeding RM840 per month. This income is derived from active involvement in the Well-Being Farm which was the main income source. However, there were still poor participants (4.4%).

This PLI poverty analysis thus shows a good state whereby participants' poverty could be addressed as 95.6% of participants have come out of poverty after joining the Gahai Agropolitan Project.

## 4. Conclusion

The Agropolitan project implementation as a mechanism for poverty eradication in rural area is a precise effort to eradicate poverty and subsequently be able to break the Vicious Poverty Cycle. Agropolitan project development throughout Malaysia is a recognition of Malaysian government's effort to improve socio-economic development and improve quality of life and ultimately eradicate poverty, especially in the rural areas. Toward this goal, responsible ministries and agencies, including state government, must have a mechanism in drawing up an effective program for ensuring the goals of the program can be achieved, thus providing positive impacts to participants. The Gahai Agropolitan Project case study has shown how its implementation can contribute to poverty eradication through increasing the participant's income so that they are able to move out of poverty. In the long run, poverty among the participants and their second-generation households could be eradicated through improved human capital development involving improvement in education and health facilities and sustained by institutional support that would benefit the rural community as a whole.

## Author details

Mohd Khairi Ismail[1], Chamhuri Siwar[2]* and Muhamad Zahid Muhamad[3]

1 Faculty of Business, UCSI University, Malaysia

2 Institute for Environment and Development (LESTARI), Universiti Kebangsaan, Malaysia

3 Faculty of Plantation and Agrotechnology, Universiti Teknologi MARA, Malaysia

*Address all correspondence to: csiwar@ukm.edu.my

## References

[1] Chamhuri S, Ferdoushi A, Nor D, Shaharudin I, Amelia H, Siti ZZ. Poverty mapping and assessing socio-demographic characteristics of the households: A case study in Pahang, Malaysia. Journal of Applied Sciences. 2014;**14**(20):2632-2640

[2] Kanbur R, Sumner A. Poor countries or poor people? Development assistance and the new geography of global poverty. Journal of International Development. 2012;**24**(6):686-695

[3] Ravallion M. Chapter 59 evaluating anti-poverty programs. In: Handbook of Development Economics. Amsterdam, North-Holland: Elselvier; 2007

[4] The Millennium Development Goals Report 2015. The Millennium Development Goals Report 2015. 2016

[5] Economic Planning Unit (EPU). Fifth Malaysia Plan. 1990:307. Available from: http://www.pmo.gov.my/dokumenattached/RMK/RM5.pdf

[6] Economic Planning Unit (EPU). The Fourth Malaysia Plan (FMP)/4MP 1981-1985. Fourth Malaysia Plan [Internet]. 1980:1-267. Available from: http://www.pmo.gov.my/dokumenattached/RMK/RM4.pdf

[7] Economic Planning Unit (EPU). Rancangan Malaysia Kesebelas (Eleventh Malaysia Plan): 2016-2020. 2015:1-372. Available from: http://rmk11.epu.gov.my/book/eng/Elevent-Malaysia-Plan/RMKe-11Book.pdf

[8] Shaffril HAM, Nasir AFA, Idris K, Uli J, Drsquo JL. Agriculture project as an economic development tool to boost socio-economic level of the poor community: The case of Agropolitan project in Malaysia. African Journal of Business Management. 2010;**4**(11):2354-2361

[9] Ismail MK, Siwar C, Ghazali R. Gahai agropolitan project in eradicating poverty: Multidimensional poverty index. Plan Malaysia. 2018;**16**(7):97-108

[10] Kementerian Luar Bandar dan Wilayah. Laporan Penilaian Outcome Projek Pembangunan Kementerian Luar Bandar dan Wilayah (MRRD). Putrajaya: Ministry of Rural and Regional Development, Malaysia; 2013

[11] Jomo KS, Ahmad SK. Teori Pembangunan Ekonomi: Satu Ulasan Kritis Terhadap Pendekatan Yang Sedia Ada. Kuala Lumpur, Malaysia: Utusan Publications; 2004

[12] Barke M, editor. Conceptual Frameworks in Geography: Case Study Supplements Case Studies of the Third World. London, United Kingdom: Oliver & Boyd; 1991

[13] Gill R. Economic Development: Past and Present. Englewood Cliffs, NJ: Prentice-Hall; 1963

[14] Watkins K, Carvajal L, Coppard D, Fuentes R, Ghosh A, Giamberardini C, et al. United Nations Development Program 2007. Human Development Report; 2007;**2**:70-75

[15] Matin I, Hulme D. Programs for the poorest: Learning from the IGVGD program in Bangladesh. World Development. 2003;**31**(3):647-665

[16] Sachs J. The End of Poverty: How We Can Make It Happen in Our Lifetime. United Kingdom: Penguin UK; 2005

[17] Friedmann J, Douglass M. Agropolitan development: Towards a new strategy for regional planning in Asia. In: Growth Pole Strategy and Regional Development Policy [Internet]. United Kingdom: Elsevier; 1978. pp. 163-192. Available from:

https://linkinghub.elsevier.com/retrieve/pii/B9780080219844500149

[18] Friedman JW, Weaver C. C. 1979. Territory and Function: The Evolution of Regional Planning. United Kingdom: British Library Cataloguing in Publication Data; 1989

[19] Douglass M. Agropolitan development: An alternative for regional development in Asia. Himalayan Review. 1981;**13**:37-71

[20] Hardoy JE, Satterthwaite D. Small and intermediate urban centres in the third world. What role for government? Third World Planning Review. 1988;**3**:27-43

[21] Buang A, Habibah A, Hamzah J, Ratnawati YS. The agropolitan way of re-empowering the rural poor. World Applied Sciences Journal. 2011;**13**(13):1-6

[22] Zulfa FI, Syamsul M, Endang GS, Tajuddin B, Aris M. Agroindustry based agropolitan institutional design with analytical network process. Journal Teknologi Pertanian. 2009;**19**(3):130-137

[23] Bajracharya BN. Promoting small towns for rural development: A view from Nepal. Asia-Pacific Popul J [Internet]. 1995;**10**(2):1-13. Available from: https://www.un-ilibrary.org/population-and-demography/promoting-small-towns-for-rural-development-a-view-from-nepal_f9234773-en

[24] Murdoch J. Networks - A new paradigm of rural development? Journal of Rural Studies. 2000;**16**(4)407-419

[25] Akkoyunlu S. The potential of rural–urban linkages for sustainable development and trade. Interantional Journal of Sustainable Develpoment and World Policy. 2015;**4**(2):20-40

[26] Krejcie RV, Morgan DW. Determining sample size for research activities. Educational and Psychological Measurement. 1970;**30**(3):607-610

Chapter 3

# Landscape of Enhanced Access to Social Protection, Safety Nets and Increased Resilience in Bangladesh

*Ismat Ara Begum, Rezaul Karim Talukder, Mohammad Mizanul Haque Kazal and Mohammad Jahangir Alam*

## Abstract

Social protection is an essential government investment that contributes to economic growth and makes growth more pro-poor through directly reducing poverty. The Government is strongly committed to reducing poverty, improving human development and reducing inequality. This commitment is reflected in Vision 2021, the Perspective Plan 2010–2021 and in the Sixth & Seventh Five Year Plans. The Government realizes that notwithstanding the past impressive progress with poverty reduction, there is a substantial number of populations that remains exposed to poverty owing to various vulnerabilities. Evidence shows that the poor and vulnerable group cannot cope with all the frequently occurring risks and shocks with their own resources. In recognition of these concerns, the Government has embarked upon the formulation of a comprehensive National Social Security Strategy. It builds on the past rich experience and seeks to streamline and strengthen the existing safety net programs. It also broadens the scope of Social Security from the narrow safety net concept to include employment policies and social insurance to address the emerging needs. Given this backdrop, this chapter deals with the assessment of social security interventions against Life Cycle Risks, measures for resilience of safety net programs, and finally presents the government priorities based on existing policies.

**Keywords:** landscape, social protection, safety nets, increased resilience, Bangladesh

## 1. Introduction

### 1.1 Social protection and poverty in Bangladesh

Bangladesh is one of the world's most densely populated countries where 1063 person live in each square kilometer of land [1]. Ever since its independence, Bangladesh has been known as one of the world's poorest countries although recently the country has transformed into lower middle income one [2]. Every year the country has been facing problems of flood, deforestation due to over population, erosion and natural calamities. The earliest Household Income and Expenditure Survey (HIES) in 1973/74 showed that 71% population lived below the poverty line. However, the picture changed quite significantly with the pace of time. Poverty reduction in Bangladesh has been significant but modest since the 1990s. The poverty trend shows notable progress, it was 52%, 44% and 31.5% in 2000, 2005 and 2010, respectively. Although poverty rate declined by 1.7% per annum at national level, currently still 23.5% of households in the country live in poverty [3]. That means, a total of 37.6 million people is still poor including 19.4 million extreme poor [4]. Gini Co-efficient was 0.458 in 2010 compared to 0.467 in 2005, indicating little improvement in income inequality [5]. Despite Bangladesh's remarkable progress of lifting 16 million people out of poverty in the past decade, poverty remains a stubborn problem. The most crucial challenge threatening Bangladesh is eliminating this widespread poverty. However, the government is strongly committed to reducing poverty and lowering inequality. This commitment is reflected in Vision 2021 through the Perspective Plan of Bangladesh 2010–2021 where poverty will be drastically reduced, citizens will be able to meet every basic need and development will be on fast track with accelerated rate of economic growth through social protection and social inclusion of marginal people in its development effort. Moreover, the government in its development agenda aspires to transform Bangladesh economy to a middle-income country by 2021. With this end in view, the government has predominantly emphasized poverty eradication in its development strategy to reduce the poverty rate from 23.5% in 2016 to 15% by 2021.

In this regard, Bangladesh has found many kinds of mechanisms and strategies. Social protection program is one of mechanisms and strategies. Social protection is an essential government investment that contributes to economic growth and makes growth more pro-poor and inclusive through directly reducing poverty. Social protection encompasses the instruments which has been used to tackle chronic and shock induced poverty and vulnerability of the poor and marginalized population. Social protection facilitates the poor to cope with shocks to their incomes by improving coverage, timeliness and scale. Social protection also strengthens disaster prevention and mitigation strategies. In addition, social protection includes social insurance such as health insurance as well as labor market programs [2].

Social protection programs are crucial part of Bangladesh's poverty reduction strategies. In this regard, major policy documents such as Sustainable Development Goals (SDGs), Seventh Five Year Plan (7FYP) and previously, Poverty Reduction Strategy Papers recognize the importance of social protection programs in supporting livelihoods and food security of the poor and also protect the poor households from poverty and vulnerability. The government of Bangladesh (GoB) aims to develop various kinds of effective social protection policies and programs to address poverty and vulnerability of its population and allocated around US$ 3 billion to support these programs [6]. These programs include safety nets, social insurance (e.g., pensions, unemployment) and labor market programs [7]. All these social protection programs intend to facilitate education, health, vulnerability reduction, employment creation, risk reduction etc. [8].

#### *1.1.1 Policies and progress to date: social protection and safety net programs (SNPs)*

As a protective mechanism for the poor, social protection has a long history since Ancient Egypt and the Roman Empire. The concept was later popularized in East Asia during the financial crisis [9]. In the context of the developing world, social protection is relatively a new term that expands from the concept of short-term safety net programs and emphasizes a longer-term development approach, which includes social assistance and insurance [10].

Bangladesh, after liberation in 1971, was desperately poor, vulnerable, and densely populated with an agrarian economy subject to frequent natural disasters. Therefore, eliminating widespread poverty was the most crucial challenge. Only two programs e.g. food rations and relief works were considered as social safety net programs for preventing the poverty as well as shocks of the victims. In response to the devastating famine of 1974, the first round of innovations took place, the World Food Program (WFP) initiated the Vulnerable Group Feeding (VGF) Program in 1975 due to 1974 famine in Bangladesh [11]. At that time food-for-work was momentously scaled-up and the Grameen experiment with micro-credit took off. Second round of innovation took place in the late 1980s. The response to consecutive floods of 1987 and 1988, there were these two innovations. Workfare innovation that combining goals of road maintenance, social forestry and women empowerment were launched at that time. Conditional cash transfers (CCTs) were launched in the form of food-for-education program in the early 1990s. School enrolment and attainment among children was quite low, especially among girls at the secondary level until the early 1990s. In the late 1990s allowance programs took off focusing on elderly and vulnerable women. During the 1990s, there was significant investment by donors in various programs managed by NGOs, provided a range of social services, including social transfers. The programs were broadening with focus to combine 'protection' and 'promotion' goals in early 2000s. In the late 2000s,

| Time period | Innovations | Contextually Relevant Factors |
|---|---|---|
| Mid to late 1970s | VGF scaled-up FFW<br>Micro-credit | Innovations in response to the food shortage of 1974 |
| Mid 1980s | VGF transformed to VGD (later to IGVGD) to re-orient focus from relief to relief + development | There were concerns that feeding alone was not enough to reduce chronic poverty/hunger and that poor were needed to be brought under the new initiatives of being given training for income-generating activities. |
| Late 1980s | **RMP:** Workfare innovations<br>- adding promotional goals to protection goals - extending workfare projects beyond earth-work e.g. social forestry, road maintenance | Innovations in response to the devastation of consecutive floods of 1987 and 1988 which required new policy emphasis on all-weather infrastructure in place of seasonal earthen infrastructure. |
| Early 1990s | **CCTs:** Food-for Education Program | Introduction of Food for Education and Female School Stipend Program was driven by two contextual factors:<br>i. a political factor contingent upon the return of parliamentary democracy in 1991 that saw elected leaders seeking new sources of political support;<br>ii. an instrumental search for new use of food aid on the phasing out of Palli Rationing program |
| Late 1990s | VGF Card<br>Old Age Allowance<br>Widow Allowance | VGF card was an innovation occasioned by the devastating flood of 1998 when rapid deployment of a food security program was urgently necessary.<br>The two allowance programs were innovations driven by competitive populist politics |

| Time period | Innovations | Contextually Relevant Factors |
|---|---|---|
| Early 2000s | **Graduation goals**<br>A series of successor programs to RMP and VGD with more explicit combination of protection and promotional goals | A discourse shift from protection goals to protection + promotion goals |
| Mid 2000s | **Geographic Targeting**<br>Monga, chars | Greater recognition of poverty pockets |
| Late 2000s | **Employment Guarantee** | The food price hike of 2007–2008 spurred a new initiative that saw a major innovation in terms of introduction of employment guarantee (bulk employment during slack seasons) in workfare program |
| Early 2010s | a. Cash Transfer (Allowances) Programs<br>b. Miscellaneous Funds: Social Empowerment/protection<br>c. Development Sector Programs: Social Empowerment | (a) Ration for Shaheed Family and Injured Freedom Fighters<br>(b)<br>• Rehabilitation and creation of alternative employment for people engaged in begging<br>• Universal Pension Insurance Scheme<br>• Construction of Sweeper Colony at district and<br>• Metropolitan cities<br>• Program on the Uplift of Harijana, Dalit, Bade, Tran's Gender (Hijra) and the embers of oppressed section of the society<br>(c)<br>• Regional Fisheries and Livestock Development Projects undertaken for fisheries development such as Jatka (Fish) protection and alternative employment for fishermen<br>• Post Literacy Education Project for human resource development<br>• One Household One Farm<br>• Revitalization of Community Health Care Initiative in Bangladesh<br>• Female Stipend for Degree (Pass) and Equivalent Level<br>• Community Based Health Care<br>• Maternal, Child, Reproductive and Adolescent Health (MCRAH)<br>• Food and Livelihood Security<br>• Creation of employment and self-employment opportunities for unemployed youths in 7 districts<br>• Integrated Rural Employment Support Project for the Poor Women<br>• Employment Opportunities of Char Dwellers in Greater Rangpur Districts through Sugarcane Cultivation |

| Time period | Innovations | Contextually Relevant Factors |
|---|---|---|
| Mid 2010s | a. Cash Transfer: Social Protection<br>b. Social Empowerment<br>c. Miscellaneous Funds: Social Protection | a. Program for Livelihood Improvement of tea-garden laborers<br>b. Trust for the protection of the persons with neuro-developmental disabilities<br>• Welfare Trust for Physical disabilities<br>• Joyeeta Foundation<br>a. Women's Skill Based Training for Livelihood<br>• Street Children Rehabilitation Program<br>• Promotion of Services & Opportunity to the Disabled Person in Bangladesh<br>• Strengthening Public Financial Management for Social Protection |

*Source: [3, 14].*

**Table 1.**
*Evolution of social protection and social safety net in Bangladesh.*

a prominent focus was geographic targeting. Until 2002, cash for education program was named as a food for education. In 2002, this program was terminated and replaced by the Primary Education Stipend Program (PESP). Now the objectives of this PESP are to increase enrolment from poor families, reduce drop-out, increase rate of completion, control child labor and raise quality of primary education [12].

However, according to the classification used by the Ministry of Finance of the GoB, the major social SNPs in Bangladesh are divided under two broad categories: (i) social protection measures; (ii) social empowerment measures. By another typology, SNPs can be also divided into four broad categories: (i) employment generation programs, (ii) programs to cope with natural disasters and other shocks, (iii) incentives to parents for children's education, and (iv) incentives to the families to improve their living status. These four broad categories can be divided into two types on the basis of mode of payment: (a) cash transfer, including conditional cash transfer (Food-for-Education Program, PESP, Female Secondary School Assistance Project, Old Age Allowance (OAA), and Rural Maintenance Program (RMP)); and (b) food transfer (Food-for Work Program, Vulnerable Group Development (VGD) Program, VGF Program, Test Relief (TR) and Gratuitous Relief (GR)) [13]. The general progression of social protection and safety net has been portrayed in **Table 1** with the contextually relevant factors.

Past mechanism/delivery system was not fully appropriate for the real poor people. For example, land criteria, were widely used to distinguish between the poor and the non-poor but evidence from the HIES suggests these criteria could lead to significant misallocation of resources. Land ownership by itself, then, was not an especially useful criterion. Ahmed [15] found that almost 47% of beneficiaries of the PESP were non-poor and incorrectly included. However, the criteria may not be appropriate and can lead to exclusion errors – i.e., some poor are classified as non-poor and cannot gain access to the programs. Programs are captured by elite members in the community who select beneficiaries and can crowd out voiceless members of the community. Using the Food for Education program as an example, [16] found considerable evidence of local capture e.g. the benefits were less likely to reach those who came from female headed, widowed or landless families. Moreover, the women concerned held major assets prior to joining VGD, had a diversified income and were more likely to have husbands with an income earning status.

Some recipients of the OAA appeared to be below the age of eligibility. False prioritization (high inclusion error) was found – excluded respondents reported that the selection process was not proper. Some percentage of beneficiaries had to adopt unfair means to be inducted in the program and in some cases, they received less than the allotted amount. A PERC report showed that a large part of budgetary allocation for the female secondary stipend program (about 20–40%) did not reach to the beneficiaries. There was weak capacity to both administer and monitor the system – often leading to leakages and inefficient targeting of beneficiaries.

However, the ministries recognize that their staff – and local government staff – needs significant capacity development to be able to manage schemes effectively and properly. In this regard, the Bangladesh Bureau of Statistics (BBS) has taken an endeavor to establish a Bangladesh Poverty Database using the Proxy Means Test approach. Monetizing benefits is already an important development in Bangladesh. Recently, the mobile banking plays an important role for the poor village people, it gives them easy access to the allocated money. Moreover, the voucher program and 'Food Card' managed by the Ministry of Food, being piloted to reduce maternal/child mortality, provide an immediate transfer to the poor. Households targeted based on criteria that are most closely related to occupation and income are more effective than those selected on the basis of assets such as land. Besides, in case of conditional cash transfer, cash is being transferred to beneficiaries' guardians/beneficiaries bank accounts. In case of emergency or seasonal relief, food transfer by the public food distribution system and in case of public works or training-based cash or in-kind transfer, food transferred by the public food distribution system and cash transferred by the public sector banks are some of the special arrangements.

In this era of digital technology automated system can maintain and regularly update the Social Safety Nets beneficiaries by program and transfers payments which can simplify SSS implementation, lower transaction costs, and minimize corruption. There is no database of beneficiaries. In the recent past the government is taking necessary steps to effectively manage and monitor the social security programs and strengthening the delivery systems for priority transfers by establishing advanced MIS and trained professional staff. Besides, the government is expanding the awareness of the social security programs for the beneficiaries and motivating potential contributors.

### *1.1.2 Coverage of social protection and social safety net programs in Bangladesh and adopting life cycle approach in NSSS*

A variety of the social safety net programs are being implemented in many countries across the world to sever the underserved people as means of 'protection' as well as 'promotion' [17]. In Bangladesh due to the high incidence of shocks and the large number of vulnerable populations, the government has raised social safety net expenditure since the mid-1990s. Annual outlay on safety net programs amounted to US$ 1.64 billion which was approximately 1.6% of national GDP in 2011 [18]. In the national budget of 2016–2017, the government allocated 2.19% of GDP for social protection.

#### *1.1.2.1 Life cycle approach*

The approaches of social protection are poor relief approach, lifecycle approach and social risk management approach of the World Bank. The poor relief approach is a short-term planning striving to resolve poverty immediately by investing limited per capita resources. It was started from Europe in 19th century and later spread out in some developing countries including Bangladesh. Due to large targeting errors and small budgets it has no focus on comprehensively tackling poverty. The World Bank developed social risk management approach (SRM) for protecting basic livelihood and promoting risk taking extending social protection to include prevention, mitigation and coping strategies focusing on the poor and vulnerable people in the 1990s. The lifecycle approach reflects that individuals face different risks and vulnerabilities at different stages in life. It has been designed to address risks at each stage providing basic social protection to citizens from the cradle to the grave. This approach was adopted some European countries like Sweden in the twentieth century and was introduced UK in 1945 and subsequently used across developed countries and also in a range of developing countries. The approach focuses resources on particular lifecycle risks in a more comprehensive manner with long term planning and programmes. Bangladesh has adopted the lifecycle approach to social protection in the National Social Security Strategy (NSSS).

The social security systems innovated to address the risks and challenges associated with across the lifecycle. So, lifecycle approach provides a comprehensive framework of lifecycle of a human being and analyses the basic risks along with the cycle. The major stages in the lifecycle mapping of human being are early childhood, school age, youth, working age and old age. Besides, pregnancy period of women is a special stage of lifecycle. Based on the lifecycle mapping, most of the existing social security programmes of Bangladesh fit in the lifecycle framework even though this was not used explicitly as a strategic consideration. Thus, the lifecycle based social protection system is promoting to consolidate the fragmented social safety net programmes into lifecycle framework. The Action Plan Implementation of NSSS of Bangladesh under the guideline of NSSS has brought in a paradigm shift in the social security programmes of Bangladesh. The Action Plan delivers for the major social protection programmes to be aligned across a lifecycle framework. It has been planned to cover poor, near poor and vulnerable people to protect from the different types of shocks and disasters throughout the lifecycle including pregnant women and disables. The Action Plan for governance reforms incorporating agenda for strengthening systems of objective targeting based on poverty scores, formulation of a single registry integrated MIS, digital payment in the form of G2P, and results-based M&E [19].

A life cycle approach has been recognized as an effective means of building National Social Protection System by the World Bank [20] in its Social Protection and Labor Strategy document. A life cycle approach also underpins the approach of the Social Protection floor, which has been promoted by the United Nations and endorsed by many countries including Bangladesh [20]. The social protection floor sets out four basic social security guarantees for the elderly, people with disabilities, children and the unemployed. The SSSs of most countries gradually evolve to address the risks and challenges across the life span. An individual is being exposed to predictable or unexpected risks which vary in nature over the life course.

The poverty profile of Bangladesh in the life cycle approach is presented below:

#### *1.1.2.2 Pregnancy and early childhood*

Poverty rates in 2010 in households with children aged 0–4 years are - at 41.7%. This is much higher than national poverty rates which is 31.5% in 2010 and 24.3% using upper poverty line [21]. This indicating the challenges and additional expenses caused by having young children when mothers are unable to work and earn. When the near poor are included, around 57% of households with children aged 0–4 years could be regarded as poor or vulnerable to poverty.

*1.1.2.3 School age*

In recent years, school enrolment among poor children aged 6–10 years increased from 72% in 2005 to 78% in 2010, while among those aged 11–15 it increased from 54–70%. Around 17.5% of children aged 5–17 years are child laborers, with 24% of boys and 10% of girls. Among older children, the proportion will be much higher.

*1.1.2.4 Young people*

The main challenge faced by adolescents and young people is a lack of skills. Many do not gain sufficient secondary education and there are not enough vocational training programs available to compensate.

*1.1.2.5 Working age population*

In 2016 Labor Force Survey, while unemployment rate is 4.2%, some 7.4% of the employed are working less than 20 hours per week [22]. This means Bangladesh has competitive advantage is its large labour pool which is currently under-utilized. Female labor force participation is low - at 36% - compared to 83% for men. This may reflect traditional social attitudes to women and their weak bargaining power in work.

*1.1.2.6 Disability*

Disability can happen at stage of life course- can be at early stage, productive age or old age. Around 8.9% of the total population – 8% of males and 9.3% of females – has some form of disability, although those who could be regarded as severely disabled comprise 1.5% of total population.

*1.1.2.7 Old age*

Demographic changes underway in Bangladesh mean that the population is gradually aging. Currently, around 7% of the population is over 60 years and, this will increase significantly in the coming decades, reaching almost 12% by 2030 and 23% by 2050. According to HIES 2010 some 28.2% of people aged over 60 are found below the poverty line [3]. According to the Ministry of Finance, there are 144 programs under the SSS currently financed through the budget and the total amount spent on these programs in FY2015–16 was Tk.375.46 billion [6]. Among them, the numbers of life cycle-based programs are 71. Besides, the government is pursuing some other kinds of major programs such as, emergency or seasonal relief programs, micro-credit programs, climate change related programs and food security programs. In FY 2016–2017, government intends to enhance the coverage of the social protection programs. The government intends to increase the number of beneficiaries of OAA by 5% which will raise the total number to 31.5 lac and raising the monthly allowance by Tk. 100 to Tk. 500.

## 1.2 National Social Security Strategy (NSSS) and policy targets

The government is strongly committed to reducing poverty, improving human development and reducing inequality. This commitment is reflected in Vision 2021, the Perspective Plan 2010–2021, and in the Sixth and 7th Five Year Plans covering the period 2011–2020. The government realizes that despite the past impressive progress with poverty reduction, there is a substantial population that remains exposed to poverty owing to various vulnerabilities.

The present SNPs indicates that the government's response to support the poor to manage and cope-up various vulnerabilities. Recent studies on identified the fact that although the overall coverage of the SNPs is wider, a sizeable share of the benefits go to the non-poor. This implies that inclusion error is quite high. Another recent finding, highlighted in the studies [23–26], is that safety net coverage varies significantly by region. There is considerable leakage of allocated funds [25, 26] and a significant percentage of household beneficiaries are non-poor [27–32]. Consequently, the impact on poverty reduction from these programs is much less than which was otherwise possible with better safety net system.

In recognition of these concerns, the government has embarked upon the formulation of a comprehensive NSSS [33]. It built on the past rich experience and sought to streamline and strengthen the existing SNPs in order to achieving better results on poverty reduction.

**NSSS Vision:** Build an inclusive social security system for all deserving Bangladeshis that effectively tackles and prevents poverty and inequality and contributes to broader human development, employment and economic growth.

**NSSS Goal over the Next Five Years:** Reform the NSSS by ensuring more efficient and effective use of resources, strengthened delivery systems and progress towards a more inclusive form of social security that effectively tackles lifecycle risks, prioritizing the poorest and most vulnerable members of society.

## 2. Macroeconomic policies on social safety nets

### 2.1 Social safety nets in 7th five year plan (7FYP)

The 7FYP, across fiscal years (FY) 2016–2020, begins with the aim of taking the country to the rank of a middle-income country. The 7th Plan seeks to reduce poverty rate to 18.6% and extreme poverty to around 8.9% by FY20. The main challenge for the 7th Plan in the area of social protection is the successful implementation of the NSSS. Along with growth, human development, the 7th Plan emphasized on social protection as essential elements of a comprehensive poverty reduction strategy and therefore spending on social protection to the level of 2.3% of GDP.

Food security strategy under the 7FYP are in line with the three objectives of the National Food Policy (NFP 2006) [34] and the National Food Policy Plan of Action (2008–2015) [35]. The NSSS provides a sound strategy that defines the various life-cycle based population groups (the young children, school going children, vulnerable women, the elderly and the physically challenged vulnerable population) and seeks to mitigate those risks by instituting a well-designed SNP that reaches the people below poverty line. It emphasizes tax-funded SNP with contributory social insurance and employment regulations to protect the workers. It also seeks to improve the administrative arrangements by strengthening the delivery systems, staffing and institutions, introduce modern MIS system as well as food-based transfer payments with cash-based payments using the financial sector-based government-to-person system etc.

Along with above strategies of NSSS the 7FYP also addresses the impeding factors related to nutrition and strengthen the enabling environment for scaling up nutrition. Therefore, the plan also has given attention on gender issues in nutrition programs specially malnutrition among children and women. Moreover, Iron-folic acid supplementation among pregnant, lactating women and adolescent girls to cover iron-deficiency anemia are also undertaken. The 7FYP intends to expand coverage of core schemes for the extreme/hard-core poor, marginalized and most vulnerable people of the society, focusing on mother and child, youth, working age, the elderly and people with disabilities and vulnerable residents of urban areas.

Bangladesh has instituted a large number of social SNPs. However, the effectiveness of the safety net schemes is considerably lower than the potential level. The implementation of the NSSS will be a major initiative for reducing extreme poverty. There are some specialized line Ministries such as Ministry of Social Welfare, Ministry of Women and Children Affairs, Ministry of Disaster Management and Relief, and Ministry of Liberation War Affairs oversee and provide specific services to support gender equality, social inclusion and social protection. The budget allocations for these line ministries are shown in **Table 2**.

## 2.2 Social protection and safety nets in sustainable development goals (SDGs)

A total of 47 SDG targets can be identified corresponding to the 9 social protection related sectors in Bangladesh. These include child-right establishment in the due time and child-labor reduced to half, violence against women reduced to 75%, child dropout reduced to 10% by creating 100% education facility, allocation for technical and training sector in the total allocation of the education sector raised to 20%, poverty eradication, education and health issues, child mortality and maternal mortality, gender equality etc.

Some specific targets under the major relevant goals can be highlighted as under:

**SDGs Goal 1:** End poverty in all its forms everywhere.

Target 1.1. By 2030, eradicate extreme poverty for all people everywhere, currently measured as people living on less than $1.25 a day.

Actions to achieve the SDG targets during 7FYP (2016–2020)

- The 7FYP aims to reduce extreme poverty by about 4.0% to around 8.9% by FY2020.
- Expanded and inclusive social protection programs for the extreme poor.

Target 1.2. By 2030, reduce at least by half the proportion of men, women and children of all ages living in poverty in all its dimensions according to national definition.

Actions to achieve the SDG targets during 7FYP

- The 7FYP seeks to reduce poverty rate to 18.6% by FY2020.

| Ministry | FY2016 | FY2017 | FY2018 | FY2019 | FY2020 |
|---|---|---|---|---|---|
| Ministry of Social Welfare | 2.0 | 6.5 | 7.5 | 8.4 | 9.6 |
| Ministry of Women and Children Affairs | 1.5 | 3.7 | 4.2 | 4.7 | 5.2 |
| Ministry of Liberation War Affairs | 4.4 | 4.3 | 4.9 | 5.4 | 6.1 |
| Ministry of Food | 6.3 | 8.6 | 9.7 | 10.7 | 12.0 |
| Ministry of Disaster Management & Relief | 23.3 | 24.0 | 27.0 | 30.1 | 33.6 |
| **Sector Total** | **37.5** | **47.1** | **53.3** | **59.4** | **66.6** |

*Source: [4].*

**Table 2.**
*ADP allocation for social safety net in 7FYP (taka billion, FY2015–2016 prices).*

Target 1.3. Implement nationally appropriate social protection systems and measures for all, including floors, and by 2030 achieve substantial coverage of the poor and the vulnerable.

Actions to achieve the SDG targets during 7FYP

- Spending on social protection as a share of GDP to be increased to 2.3% by FY2020.

Actions to achieve the SDG targets during 7FYP were to

- Undertake programs on agriculture, rural infrastructure, and employment generation and for curving poverty.
- Scaling up of poverty reduction action plan for addressing poverty with lessons learnt from the relevant ongoing projects in different ministries .
- Increase spending on social protection and social inclusion from 2% of GDP in FY2015 to 2.3% in FY2020

**SDGs Goal 2:** End hunger, achieve food security and improved nutrition and promote sustainable agriculture.

**Target 2:** By 2030, end hunger and ensure access by all people in vulnerable situations, including infants, to safe, nutritious and sufficient food all year round

Actions to achieve the SDG targets during 7FYP

- Increase agriculture-product diversification and consumption for improving nutrition
- Implement Bangladesh National Nutrition Policy 2015
- Continue operational plan for National Nutrition Services under Health Sector Program
- Implement Children Act 2013 for child nutrition
- Support small and marginal farmers in producing diversified crop suitable for both markets and household consumption to improve their nutritional status.

Actions to achieve the SDG targets during 7FYP

- Enhance PES with appropriate strategies and policies for poverty reduction.

## 3. Challenges observed and successes achieved: situation updates and analysis in trends on food security and nutrition in Bangladesh

### 3.1 Social protection strategies in NSSS

A strategy for nutrition planning is outlined in the National Food Policy (2006) [34] and the National Food Policy Plan of Action – NFP PoA (2008–2015) [35], which was developed by 11-line ministries [34]. The main objectives of the NFP PoA are to achieve adequate and stable supply of safe and nutritious food for everyone, especially women and children [35]. The Institute of Public Health and Nutrition of

DGHS are the institutional home for nutrition. Nutrition program of the Ministry of Health and Family Welfare (MoHFW) has been mainstreamed within the Directorate General Health Services (DGHS) and Directorate General of Family Planning (DGFP) through a new operational plan for National Nutrition Services. Apart from MoHFW, other ministries also play important roles in improving nutrition. Ministry of Agriculture provides extension services for different crops fortification with nutrition elements, newly developed by research institutes of Bangladesh

### 3.2 Budgetary trends, allocations for social protection in public expenditure

The Ministry of Finance publishes a comprehensive list of SNPs every year with their coverage and budgetary allocations in its budget documents. The document also compares the public spending on SNPs and the total development and non-development expenditures of the government. Reflecting the government's commitment to social protection, budgetary allocations have grown in absolute terms as well as a share of GDP. The trend of allocation for social protection and social empowerment and their shares in the national budget and GDP is presented in **Table 3**. The allocation for social protection programs increased from 1.3% of GDP in 1998 to 2.3% in FY2016. Since then it has stabilized around 2% of GDP. Although this level of funding is modest by international standards, when measured against the government's tight budget situation, this represents a substantial commitment, accounting for 13% of total government spending, and reflects the high priority accorded by the government to this aspect of the social development policy. Government's spending on social protection programs in the FY 2016–2017 is 33066.62 core Taka which is 13.28% of the total budget and 2.31% of the GDP [33]. On the other hand, government's spending for the social empowerment programs is 12163.40 core Taka (3.57% of the budget and 0.62% of the GDP) in FY 2016–2017.

### 3.3 Assessment on proposed programs and sub-programs/projects

Bangladesh's current social protection system is complex, comprising a large number of programs and managed by many ministries. According to a comprehensive official compilation prepared by the Ministry of Finance, Bangladesh is implementing a total of 144 (including 10 newly added programs) SNPs according to the budget 2014–2015. These programs are classified in four different categories. These are (i) Cash Transfer (22 programs), (ii) Food Security (9 programs), (iii) Micro-Credit and Miscellaneous Funds (20 programs), (iv) Development Sector (93 programs including newly introduced 10 development programs). However, many of these programs do not qualify as social protection as well as for the purpose of calculation of social protection index. Among these, 37 programs are classified into: social protection and social empowerment which are under cash transfer, food security and development sector programs and miscellaneous funds. However, among those 37 programs, the most remarkable SNPs in progress are: Allowances for the Widow, OAA, Deserted and Destitute Women, Allowances for Financially Insolvent Persons with Disabilities, Allowances for Urban, Maternity Allowance Program for the Poor Lactating Mothers, Low-income Lactating Mothers, Grants for Residents in Government Orphanages and Other Institutions, Honorarium for Freedom Fighters, Capitation Grants for Orphan Students in Non-government Orphanages, Pension for Retired Government Employees and their Families, Ration for Shaheed Families and Injured Freedom Fighters, VGF, Block Allocation for Disaster Management, VGD, TR Food, GR. The major programs in progress are OAA, Allowance for the Disabled, Allowance for the Widowed, Deserted and Destitute Women, VGD, VGF, Freedom Fighter Allowance,

| Allocation items | 2009–2010 | 2010–2011 | 2011–2012 | 2012–2013 | 2013–2014 | 2014–2015 | 2015–16 | 2016–2017 |
|---|---|---|---|---|---|---|---|---|
| Total: (Social Protection - Taka in Core) | 13444.31 | 17237.47 | 17237.47 | 17479.98 | 18983.53 | 21529.39 | 25263.58 | 33066.62 |
| Social Protection (% to budget) | 12.16 | 10.69 | 10.69 | 9.23 | 8.78 | 8.98 | 9.55 | 9.71 |
| Social Protection (% to GDP) | 1.95 | 1.88 | 1.88 | 1.68 | 1.61 | 1.42 | 1.46 | 1.69 |
| Total: (Social Empowerment - Taka in Core) | 3261.50 | 4737.76 | 4737.76 | 5617.54 | 7670.48 | 9106.13 | 10711.47 | 12163.4 |
| Social Empowerment (% to Budget) | 2.95 | 2.94 | 2.94 | 2.97 | 3.55 | 3.80 | 4.05 | 3.57 |
| Social Empowerment (% to GDP) | 0.47 | 0.52 | 0.52 | 0.54 | 0.65 | 0.60 | 0.62 | 0.62 |
| Total: Beneficiary (Lac-man) | 591.22 | 771.18 | 771.18 | 708.64 | 770.65 | 7294.15 | 6351.93 | 5165.26 |
| Total: (Man-Month) | 261.48 | 208.79 | 208.79 | 199.24 | 151.62 | 141.28 | 133.72 | 182.05 |
| Total: (Annual Lac-Man) | 21.79 | 17.40 | 17.40 | 16.60 | 12.63 | 11.77 | 11.14 | 15.17 |
| Total: Taka (Social Protection & Empowerment in Core) | 16705.81 | 21975.23 | 21975.23 | 23,097.52 | 26,654.01 | 30,636 | 35,975 | 45,230 |
| Total Budget | 110,523 | 161,213 | 161,213 | 189,326 | 216,222 | 239,668 | 264,565 | 340,605 |
| Percentage to Budget | 15.12 | 13.63 | 13.63 | 12.20 | 12.33 | 12.78 | 13.60 | 13.28 |
| GDP | 691,087 | 914,784 | 914,784 | 1,037,987 | 1,181,000 | 1,513,600 | 1,729,567 | 1,961,017 |
| Percentage to GDP | 2.42 | 2.40 | 2.40 | 2.23 | 2.26 | 2.02 | 2.08 | 2.31 |

*Source: [6].*

**Table 3.**
*Budget allocation and expenditure on social protection programs.*

Stipend for Secondary and Higher Secondary Students, PSEP, Stipend for Disabled Students, Maternity Allowance, Freedom Fighter Allowance etc. [17].

A strategic review of the social safety net programs by life cycle shows that although about 65% of the programs are seeking to address life-cycle related risks and vulnerabilities, there are serious gaps remain. For example, programs for addressing pregnancy and early childhood and old age risks have low coverage (excluding the government service pensions). Similarly, programs for addressing the disability challenges are very small. Bangladesh will face new challenges such as an aging population, increasing rural–urban migration and growing urbanization. The social security system needs to address these new challenges to keep the risks and vulnerabilities at minimum as possible, and potentially to eradicate the risks and vulnerabilities.

In the social protection programs, there is a dominance of food-security related and rural employment programs. With rapid GDP growth over the past 10 years along with good agricultural performance the incidence of hunger and food poverty is being reduced substantially. There is also evidence that labor market in agriculture is tightening as reflected in growing agricultural real wages. In view of this changing economic and agriculture landscape, nature of poverty and the risk profile is also changing, with remaining pockets of poverty in the country. These are char, haor, coastal belt, hill districts etc. These pockets of poverty area cannot reap the fruits of the country's economic progress in the last decade. This clearly indicates that the policy makers require a careful review of the adequacy of the present social protection to meet the social security requirements of Bangladesh's population in the 21st Century.

Many social protection programs focus on addressing the risks faced by the rural poor in the country. With the evolving economic transformation where both the GDP and employment share of the rural economy is declining and the urban economy is growing with an increasing concentration of poor and vulnerable population in the urban slums, the social security system needs to strategically anticipate these changing economic and social dynamics and develop programs that address the risks and the vulnerability irrespective of areas.

There is significant room for improving the effectiveness of social protection programs. In addition to consolidation and simplification of programs noted earlier, a careful approach to program design and beneficiary selection that aims to increase the participation of the poor and vulnerable and exclude the non-poor will be an important challenge for the new NSSS. A related issue is that the adequacy of attention to marginalized and excluded groups such as vulnerable women, people with disabilities, homeless, high risk groups including people living with HIV/AIDS, dalits, displaced and street children. Absence of monitoring and evaluation (M&E) is a major shortcoming of the present social protection system. There is no regular formal mechanism for reviewing the performance either at the national level or by individual programs. Different studies of the impact of a few programs which were supported by donors, have shown that there is a value of conducting regular M&E. The lack of a results-based M&E system is associated with the emergence of large numbers of programs, hence results based M&E can play an important role in helping the government strengthen and improve its SSS based on performance against specified quantitative targets.

### 3.4 Impact assessment of social security interventions against life cycle risks

Social protection systems are established, not only to tackle poverty, but to provide families with protection against the challenges, shocks and crises that make them susceptible to falling into or go deeper into poverty [33]. Families are vulnerable to a range of crises which can hit at any time, such as ill health or covariate shocks such as natural disasters or economic recessions. These crisis and risks are being faced by individuals across the life cycle -from birth to old age.

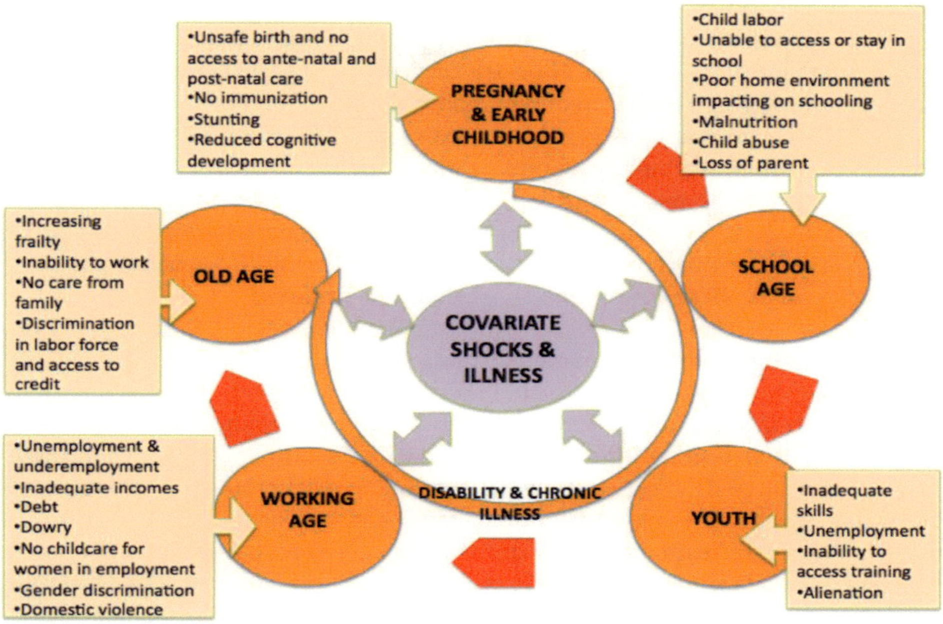


**Figure 1.**
*Life cycle risks. Source: [3].*

The social protection systems gradually evolve to address the risks and challenges across the life cycle. In essence, countries shape their social protection systems to provide support to various demographic groups, although most countries also have a small safety net to address covariate risks or need additional support.

The life cycle framework illustrates the risks faced by a citizen at different stages of the life cycle (**Figure 1**). The poverty profile analysis shows that many existing social programs of Bangladesh fit in the life cycle framework even though this was not used explicitly as a strategic consideration. But the analysis also shows there are major concerns.

A more strategic and analytically elegant way of looking at the structure of the current programs is to classify them in the context of a life cycle framework [33]. The poor and near poor population face shocks and challenges at different stages of the life cycle. Some of the underlying risks if not addressed on time could have life-lasting negative impacts. For example, the special health care needs of a mother during pregnancy and delivery or childcare need during infancy (age 0–2) if not managed well could easily jeopardize the infant's wellbeing for the entire life span. Similarly, the vulnerabilities faced by a poor old person (age 65+) are much more challenging than those faced by a poor person during the working age cycle. A social protection system that recognizes these differences in risks at different stages of the life cycle and seeks to address them will likely provide a more effective support system than one that does not specifically respond to the needs of the life cycle related risks.

## 4. Developing investment strategy for efficient management of social protection programs

### 4.1 Priority programs for investment strategy based on life-cycle approach

The NSSS strengthen the transformation towards a lifecycle system by consolidating programs in a small number of priority schemes [33]. The aim is to identify the high priority schemes and make the system more inclusive by incorporating a higher proportion of poor and vulnerable people within it. This will be achieved by gradually increasing coverage of priority schemes and ensuring that selection processes prioritize the inclusion of poor and vulnerable families.

The life cycle programs are considered as programs for early childhood and school age children, working age group, working age adults with disabilities, old age and missing programs for working age group. The life cycle programs have been identified in several dimensions of investment for food security and nutrition in Bangladesh. Investment priorities have been shown in **Table 4** according to the different social protection programs throughout the life cycle.

## 4.2 Priority programs for investment strategy

Investment in social protection in Bangladesh will contribute to the wider program's focus on economic growth and poverty reduction. It will do this through the pursuit of three strategic objectives: (1) improve social protection coverage, (2) improve the quality of social protection systems, and (3) enhance partner governments' ability to make their own informed choices about social protection options. Priority areas of engagement will be in two broad areas: (1) refining and developing social protection systems, and (2) strengthening partner government and other stakeholders' knowledge on social protection.

In Bangladesh, evidence suggests that social exclusion is strongly related to poverty, where ethnic minorities, people living in disadvantaged geographical areas and women in particular face social exclusion, resulting in fewer economic prospects and higher levels of poverty [36]. Based on evidence of performance of the on-going programs, investment strategy should be prepared to give priority on

| Stages of Life Cycles | Programs | Challenges | Investment strategies |
|---|---|---|---|
| Pregnancy & Early Childhood | 1. MCRAH<br>2. Revitalization of Community Healthcare Initiative | • Coverage is very minimal<br>• Less emphasize on nutrition<br>• Selection process is not unbiased and prerogative | • Coverage should be expanded by allocating more funds.<br>• Under nutrition problem may be taken consideration to design the program.<br>• More new programs are to be added to shelter pregnancy and early childhood risks and vulnerability. |
| School Age | 1. Primary Education Stipend<br>2. School Feeding Programs and School Feeding Programs in Poverty Prone Areas<br>3. Stipend and Access Increase for Secondary and Higher Secondary Level Students | • Around 24% of primary school age children and 17% of secondary school age children are getting primary education stipend<br>• Support for children with disabilities is minimal<br>• Girls are receiving higher than the boys<br>• Geographical and environment fragile areas are needed more attention | • Increase size of the transfers<br>• Evidence based learning programs are to be introduced to develop innovative capacity at the school age<br>• Coverage must be expanded emphasizing geographical and environmental fragile areas.<br>• Institutional capacity development investment is to given priority.<br>• Disabilities children facilities to be expanded through developing proper caring and training funding. |

| Stages of Life Cycles | Programs | Challenges | Investment strategies |
|---|---|---|---|
| Working Age | 1. Allowances for the Widow, Deserted and Destitute Women<br>2. Economic Empowerment of the Poor<br>3. Food Assistance for Chittagong Hill Tracts<br>4. Employment Generation Program for the Ultra Poor<br>5. Vulnerable Group Development<br>6. Food for Work<br>7. Social Development Foundation<br>8. Rural Employment & Road Maintenance Program<br>9. One Household One Farm<br>10. Ashrayan-2 Project | • Multiplicity of the programs<br>• Lack of coordination among the implementing agency<br>• Self-employment and capacity development related programs are not accessible<br>• Limited scope for employment generation activities<br>• Little space to work of widow, deserted and destitute women<br>• Mostly rural based program while urban employment scheme is ignored for urban vulnerable people | • Establish a Ministry of Social Development according to suggestion in NSSS for avoiding coordinating problem<br>• Evidence based employment generation programs will be funded more<br>• Self-employment and capacity development programs should be incorporated for funding<br>• Urban based employment generation program to be included for financing<br>• Effective institutionalization process to be strengthened for efficiently functioning, monitoring and evaluation the social protection programs |
| Old Age | 1. Construction of Residence for Landless and Poor Freedom Fighters<br>2. Honorarium for Insolvent Freedom Fighters<br>3. Pension for Retired Government Employees and their Families<br>4. OAA | • Not accessible to all elder people<br>• Only option is pension scheme<br>• Absence of unemployment insurance and injured worker's insurance programs<br>• Transfer amount is very low | • Health related programs should be designed for financing<br>• Unemployed and injured worker's insurance programs are to be included<br>• Expand the coverage for old age scheme<br>• OAA is to be increased |
| Disability | 1. Allowance for the Financially Insolvent Disabled | • The grant is very low<br>• Coverage is small area<br>• Lack of fairness in the selection process | • Disability grant should be increased<br>• Coverage must be nation wide<br>• Institutional capacity must be strengthened |
| General Purpose | 1. Fund for Climate Change<br>2. National Service<br>3. Block Allocation for Disaster Management<br>4. Block Allocations for Various Programs | • Difficulties associated with prompt response in climate change and disaster management | • Block allocation is necessary to increase for timely response against climate change and disaster management. |

| Stages of Life Cycles | Programs | Challenges | Investment strategies |
|---|---|---|---|
| Food Transfers | 1. VGF | • Difficult to give back up for emergency need<br>• Low coverage and transfers | • The program is important to meet urgent needs<br>• More risk prone and vulnerable areas are to taken under these programs. |
| | 2. TR Food | | |
| | 3. GR Food | | |
| | 4. Open Market Sales | | |

**Table 4.**
*Investment strategies based on major life cycle stages.*

food security and nutrition in the Second Country Investment Plan (2016–2020) of Bangladesh. For mitigating the future challenges in NSSS, different types of social protection programs are needed to expand the coverage for protecting from shocks, disabilities and vulnerabilities.

## 4.3 Government priorities based on existing policies

The NSSS provides a sound strategy that defines the various life-cycle based risks faced by the poor and vulnerable population and seeks to mitigate those by instituting a well-designed income transfer system that reaches the poorest and most vulnerable segment of the population (infants and young children, school going children, vulnerable women, elderly and the disabled) [33]. People living in remote and disadvantaged areas also deserve to be covered by the social security system. The priority challenges in the implementation of the new SSS as identified in the 7FYP include: (i) effective shift from the current discretionary to targeted universal approach to avoid leakage and under coverage, (ii) expanding coverage of the core schemes to reach the intended groups: mother and children, youth, the elderly and people with disabilities, (iii) initiating a social insurance system that enables people to invest in their own social security, (iv) strengthening the delivery systems for priority transfers by establishing advanced MIS and trained professional staff.

## 4.4 Proposed focus and priority interventions

a. Increase and modernize food storage and handling facilities, especially in disaster prone areas in the country: One priority intervention is to building of modern storage facilities that are better equipped to adapt to the climate change impacts and resist disaster shocks, repair and rehabilitation of existing warehouses and improving ambient environment of stocks to maintain quality and increase shelf life. Some progress has been made with respect to building of public storage facility development. Efforts are under way to develop household level storage facilities through use of mini silos on which some piloting has been done. Scaling up of such facilities is a priority area of intervention.

b. Strengthen institutional capacities to effectively operate the old and newly emerging social security programs: Capacities should be strengthened to develop a multi-year strategy to improve the targeting performance of SSNs, streamline and coordinate these SNPs. Attempts should also be made to improve synergies between safety net programs (food or cash for work) with productive infrastructure such as irrigation, rural transport and markets.

c. Adopt measures for disaster response and mitigation (emergency food distribution, agricultural rehabilitation): The GoB has already placed increased emphasis on the reduction of human, economic and environmental costs of disasters, through enhancing the national capacity for disaster mitigation. These efforts need to be strengthened with particular focus on agriculture-related risks and disasters.

d. Expand and strengthen programs for supporting women, children, elderly and disable persons: The NSSS will strengthen the transformation towards a life cycle system by consolidation of programs into a smaller number of priority schemes. A range of socially excluded population that faces various social discriminations based on religion, gender, age, ethnicity, profession and illness will also be brought under the social security network. The food-based programs can be made nutrition-sensitive by expanding distribution of micronutrient-fortified rice and *atta*. For improving child nutrition and school attendance of children, school feeding has proved to be an effective program which can be scaled up to a significant extent.

e. Expand and strengthen programs for supporting people living in vulnerable and disadvantaged areas: Char land, River bank, Haor, Hill tracts: The physical geography of Bangladesh is varied and consists of a broad deltaic plain having preponderance of frequent floods, soil erosion and siltation. During abnormal flooding, people fall in distress which is exacerbated by river erosion. People living in Char lands particularly struggle with floods and river erosion. Efforts have been made to reduce extreme poverty in the riverine islands of the northwestern areas through the Char Livelihood Program. Such efforts need to be scaled up by covering more geographical areas and increasing the number of beneficiaries. There are also a few programs targeted towards the ethnic communities of the Chittagong Hill Tract region which also need to be scaled up in terms of reaching the relatively inaccessible areas.

f. Invest in Employment and Income Generation Programs with focus on Productive Safety Net programs: There are as many as 8 workfare schemes of which the two largest programs are Employment Generation Program for the Poorest and Food for Work Program. The two missing areas of social security for working age group are the unemployment insurance program and the injured workers' insurance scheme. The lack of any social insurance is more pronounced in the informal sector which accounts for 87.5% of all employment [3]. These aspects need to be paid due attention in reforming the present social security system.

## 5. Conclusions

To deal with risks, poverty and vulnerabilities faced by the marginalized population groups, different SNPs have been undertaken by the government. However, the programs are predominantly rural-based, although the country is getting rapidly urbanized with an increasing proportion of the urban poor living in informal settlements such as slums.

The employment-generation programs have generated additional employment. Other benefits of such programs include improved agricultural production, enhanced marketing opportunities, reduced physical damages, loss of human lives, improved transportation and communication. Building different public infrastructure such as rehabilitation of embankments and canals, development of water bodies and improvement of rural roads have also contributed to employment generation and income growth. Over the long run, these programs contribute to food security, both at the household and national levels. However, several problems with such programs limit the potential benefits, including weak program management, considerable leakage, problems with selection of beneficiaries and types of work done, delays in fund disbursement, and weak monitoring and supervision. The various stipend projects led to increased school enrolment and minimization of gender gap.

The major emphasis should be given on those SNPs which address the long-term obstacles to economic development as well as contribute to development of human capital such as the public works program, female scholarship programs and child nutrition programs. Also, there should be carefully designed targeted transfers and credit programs for disaster-affected households and individuals. Problems with targeting and leakage should be duly addressed. Instead of using size of landholding as the criteria for selection of beneficiaries, other criteria such as occupation and other household assets need to be given priority. Leakage could be reduced through cash payment rather than in kind transfers which increase program cost. There should be improvements in the quality of basic health and education services, thereby reducing dropout rates among the poor. If the government's commitment of poverty reduction to 15% is to be taken into reality by 2021, there is a need for additional resources for the social protection programs. A part of it can come through leakage reduction from better targeting and reducing inclusion error aimed at improving the overall program efficiency, and thereby reducing system loss. Bangladesh encumbered with high incidence of poverty and underemployment, and very low levels and coverage of social protection that would need to focus on a revitalized policy intervention to move towards a full-employment goal. It is prerequisite to be make sure that projects and programmes last long enough to ensure long-lasting to support for alleviating poverty enhancing the SNPs at all level of life cycle. Policy makers and those responsible for projects implementation must consider financial, human and institutional capacities while designing projects and programs.

## Acknowledgment

This chapter was derived from the background paper entitled 'Enhanced access to social protection, safety nets and increased resilience' prepared under the 'The meeting the undernutrition challenge (MUCH) project (GCP/BGD/059/USA)'. The MUCH is being implemented by the Food and Agriculture Organization (FAO) of the United Nations and the Food Planning and Monitoring Unit, Ministry of Food with the financial support of EU and USAID.

## Author details

Ismat Ara Begum[1], Rezaul Karim Talukder[2], Mohammad Mizanul Haque Kazal[3] and Mohammad Jahangir Alam[4]*

1 Department of Agricultural Economics, Bangladesh Agricultural University, Bangladesh

2 Former National Poverty and Social Protection Policy Adviser, FAO/Ministry of Food, Dhaka, Bangladesh

3 Department of Development and Poverty Studies, Sher-e-Bangla Agricultural University, Bangladesh

4 Department of Agribusiness and Marketing, Bangladesh Agricultural University, Bangladesh

*Address all correspondence to: alambau2003@yahoo.com; mjahangir.alam@bau.edu.bd

## References


[1] BBS. Statistical Pocket Book Bangladesh 2015, Statistics Division, Ministry of Planning, Dhaka, Bangladesh

[2] World Bank. The State of Social Safety Nets 2015, Washington DC, USA.

[3] GED National Social Security Strategy (NSSS) of Bangladesh, (2015). Planning Commission, GoB, Dhaka.

[4] GED 7th Five Year Plan FY2016 - FY2020, Accelerating Growth, Empowering Citizens, 2015. Planning Commission, GoB, Dhaka.

[5] Bangladesh Economic Review (BER, 2011). Finance Division, Ministry of Finance, Government of the People's Republic of Bangladesh.

[6] Ministry of Finance. Budget Documents FY 2014-15, FY 2015-16, FY 2016-2017, Finance Division, GoB, 2015.

[7] World Bank. Social Safety Nets in Bangladesh: An Assessment. Bangladesh Development Series, 2006, Paper No. 9. World Bank Office, Dhaka.

[8] Ahmed, I., Jahan, N., and Zohora, F. T. Social Safety Net Programme as a Mean to Alleviate Poverty in Bangladesh. *Developing Country Studies*, 2014, 4(17):46-55.

[9] Paitoonpong, S. The meaning of social safety nets. *Journal of Asian Economics*, 2008, 19(5-6):467-473.

[10] Page, S. Vulnerable Yet, Viable: Social Protection Policies for Households Affected by HIV and AIDS. 2005, Policy Brief Series 02/05, FANRPAR, August.

[11] Hashemi, S. M. Including the Poorest: Linking Microfinance and Safety Net Programs. 2001, CGAP Occasional Paper 20, Consultative Group to Assist the Poorest, Washington DC.

[12] Begum, I. A., Alam, M. J., Haque, M.M., & Akter, S. Production Impacts of Cash Transfer and Conditional Cash Transfer Programs in Bangladesh: Propensity Score Matching Analysis. Paper Presented at the 29th International Conference of Agricultural Economists, Milan, Italy, 2015.

[13] Khuda, B. Social Safety Net Programmes in Bangladesh: A Review. Bangladesh Development Studies, 2011, 34 (2):87-108.

[14] Hossain, Z.H., Choudhury, L.A. and Khondaker, S.A. Social Safety Nets in Bangladesh, 2011, 1, Review of Issues and Analytical Inventory, Power and Participation Research Centre and United Nations Development Program, Dhaka.

[15] Ahmed, A. U. Assessing the Performance of Conditional Cash Transfer Programs for Girls and Boys in Primary and Secondary Schools in Bangladesh. 2004, Project report prepared for the World Bank, IFPRI, Washington DC.

[16] Galasso and Ravallion. Social Protection in a Crisis: Argentina's Plan *Jefes y Jefas.* 2003, World Bank Policy Research Working Paper 3165, November 2003. Washington DC.

[17] Begum, I.A., S. Akter, M.J.Alam and N.M. Rahmatullah, (2014). Social Safety Nets and Productive Outcomes: Evidence and Implications for Bangladesh, National Food Policy Capacity Strengthening Programme, FAO, Dhaka.

[18] Rahman H.Z, Choudhury L.A. "Social Safety Nets in Bangladesh." 2012, 2: Ground Realities and Policy Challenges, Process, Coverage, Outcomes, priorities, Power and

Participation Research Center and United Nations Development Programme, Dhaka

[19] Cabinet Division and General Economics Division (2019). A B C D of Social Protection in Bangladesh, Social Security Policy Support (SSPS) Programme, Cabinet Division and General Economics Division, Government of the People's Republic of Bangladesh, Dhaka.

[20] World Bank (2012). Resilience, Equity, and Opportunity: The World Bank's Social Protection and Labour Strategy 2012-2022. World Bank Report No. 73235. Washington DC.

[21] HIES (2016). Report on Household Income and Expenditure Survey 2016, Bangladesh Bureau of Statistics, Ministry of Planning, the Government of the Peoples Republic, Bangladesh, Published in June 2019.

[22] LFS (2016-17). Report on Labour Force Survey, 2016-17. Bangladesh Bureau of Statistics, Ministry of Planning, the Government of the Peoples Republic, Bangladesh, Published in January 2018.

[23] Alim, M. A., and Sulaiman, M. *Polli Shomaj* and 100-day Employment Generation Programme: Measuring the Targeting Effectiveness in Beneficiary Selection. 2009, Report, Research and Evaluation Division, BRAC, Dhaka, Bangladesh

[24] Ahmed, S. S. Delivery Mechanisms of Cash Transfer Programs to the Poor in Bangladesh. 2005, Social Protection Discussion Paper Series No. 0520.

[25] Ahmed, A., S. Rashid, M. Sharma and Zohir, S. A Study on food air leakage on Bangladesh. 2003, WFP/IFPRI Brief, Washington DC.

[26] Ahmed, A. U., and Del Ninno C. Impact Evaluation of Food for Education Program in Bangladesh. 2000, Food Management and Resource Support Project, IFPRI, Washington DC.

[27] Barakat, A., S.K.S. Gupta, A.A. Hussain, M. Rahman and F. M. Ahamad, 2013. Improving the Targeting Effectiveness of Social Safety Nets in Bangladesh, National Food Policy Capacity Strengthening Programme, FAO, Dhaka.

[28] Begum, S., and Wesumperuma D. Overview of the Old Age Allowance Programme in Bangladesh. Chapter 8, Social Protection for Older Persons Social Pensions in Asia, 2012, Edited by Sri Wening Handayani and Babken Babajanian, ADB, Metro Manila, 2012.

[29] Morshed, K.A.M., (2009). Social Safety Net Programmes in Bangladesh. UNDP, Dhaka, Bangladesh.

[30] Shaikh S.A., Narayan, A and Zaman, H. 'Are the Poor Protected? Vulnerability and the Role of Safety Nets' in the 'Breaking Down Poverty in Bangladesh' 2009, edited by Ambar Narayan and Hasan Zaman, The University Press Limited, Dhaka.

[31] Ahmed, S.S. Delivery Mechanism of Cash Transfer Programs to the Poor in Bangladesh. 2007, Social Protection Discussion Paper 0520, World Bank.

[32] Ahmed, A. U. and Del Ninno C. The food for education program in Bangladesh: an evaluation of its impact on educational attainment and food security, 2002, FCND discussion paper no. 138, Food Consumption and Nutrition Division, IFPRI, Washington DC.

[33] Cabinet Division and General Economics Division (2018). Action Plan – Implementation of National Social Security Strategy (NSSS) of Bangladesh, 2016-2021. Government of the People's Republic of Bangladesh, Dhaka.

[34] National Food Policy (2006). Ministry of Food and Disaster Management, Government of the People's Republic Bangladesh, Dhaka.

[35] National Food Policy Plan of Action - NFP PoA (2008-2015). Monitoring Report 2015. Food Planning and Monitoring Unit, Ministry of Food. Government of the People's Republic of Bangladesh, Dhaka.

[36] Sen, B and Hulme, D. Chronic Poverty in Bangladesh: Tales of Ascent, Descent, Marginality and Persistence. The State of the Poorest 2004/2005. 2004, The Bangladesh Institute of Development Studies. Dhaka

Chapter 4

# Including Smallholders with Vertical Coordination

*Linda Bitsch, Silva Atoyan, Barbara Richter, Jon Hanf and Taras Gagalyuk*

## Abstract

The current chapter demonstrates an application of the theoretical framework of vertical coordination, more specifically the application of contracting in productive partnerships, to integrate smallholders into the value chain of a specialised crop. The aim of the chapter is to derive implications for industry participants on how to integrate smallholders with vertical coordination. Therefore, we take a closer look on vertical coordination and contracting in productive partnerships. We have taken the value chain of brandy production in Armenia and used the Yerevan Brandy Company (YBC) to perform our case study, with which we can analyse vertical coordination mechanisms used by the company. Further, we want to identify factors that drive processors and smallholders to enter into contracts. Qualitative interviews were conducted with the YBC, their grape suppliers, as well as experts from related fields. We analysed the data with a qualitative content approach. Results show that the YBC uses different measures of vertical coordination, i.e., contracts and farm assistance in the form of consultancy and input supply. The company tends to use production contracts rather than pure marketing contracts, as it is actively engaged in the production process. The use of contract farming is beneficial for both the processing company and the smallholders.

**Keywords:** value chain, vertical coordination, contracting, smallholders, brandy, Armenia

## 1. Introduction

After the collapse of the Soviet Union in 1991, the whole food chains in Armenia and other Eastern European countries experienced an economic breakdown due to the beginning of the transition process. Problems occurred at the beginning of the transformation process. After land privatisation, and the liberalisation of prices and trades, the prevailing structures did not fit to the open market [1].

Disruption and instability in the supply chain from farmers to retailers had a negative impact on qualities and quantities. At the same time, changing consumer demands forced retailers and processors to adjust and improve the structure of the food chains to meet consumer demands and to overcome the supply problems. The agricultural policy could not provide frameworks and institutions fast enough to restructure the food commodity chains to guarantee stable and higher qualities as well as quantities. As a consequence, retailers and processors were engaged mainly in the approach of private-driven vertical coordination with partners along the supply chain to overcome the problems of supply disruption and minor quality [2, 3]. These structural changes and their consequences are still present today.

To adapt to the new environment, the Yerevan Brandy Company (YBC), the producer of Ararat brandies, was acquired by the international Pernod Ricard Group with French origin in 1998, shortly after the collapse of the Soviet Union.

Investments of foreign companies can cause structural changes in the agri-food sector. The requirements of the newly established procurement systems demand that suppliers can guarantee both disruption-free product flows and delivery of products of a certain quality, thus forcing domestic producers to keep up with quantity and quality demands to prevent the import of products [4].

Literature on the influence of foreign direct investment (FDI) on transition economies mentions several positive effects of FDI such as follows: (1) it facilitates economic growth [5, 6], (2) it reduces poverty [7, 8], and (3) it can induce technology transfer, technical innovation as well as enterprise restructuring [7]. Dyker points out that those investing companies have to impose their corporate organisational structures on subsidiaries or partners [9]. Those organisational structures are based on the disposition of hierarchies, lines of responsibility, the use of intra-firm e-mail systems, etc. Hanf et al. show the influence that foreign investors have taken in the development of the Armenian wine and brandy business. They use different Armenian companies, among others, the YBC [10].

This is why we take the YBC as a case study to show exemplarily how an international company manages to integrate local smallholders (grape growers) into their national and international value chains by successfully installing a procurement system by using different measures of vertical coordination.

The case of the YBC in the Armenian brandy industry can be seen as a benchmark example for other countries and their agricultural sectors where the structure of smallholders is still prevailing, too. Based on the case study, we derive implications for the participants.

The chapter is structured as follows. To show the theoretical background on integration of smallholders into value chains, the next chapter gives an overview about vertical coordination, and vertical coordination mechanisms, i.e., contracting in productive partnerships.[1] In the third chapter, background information on the Armenian wine industry is provided. The fourth chapter presents the case study results from the Yerevan Brandy Company. Finally, concluding remarks are offered.

## 2. Integration of smallholders into the value chain: vertical coordination and contracting

### 2.1 Vertical coordination

In everyday business, companies face decisions about the synchronisation of successive stages in the marketing channel from producers to consumers. Traditionally either spot market transactions or integrated processes in companies have been used. The spot market and vertical integration can be considered as classical modes, which continue to be applied in nowadays businesses.

The spot market represents the classic *buy* (on the market) decision, where the company organises the transaction directly on the market. That means, the company buys, for example, an input on the market place. In this case, individual

[1] The theoretical frame is mainly based on the published chapter “Integration of Small Farmers into Value Chains: Evidence from Eastern Europe and Central Asia” [11]. For a detailed review on vertical coordination, look into Hanf and Gagalyuk [11].

economic actors follow their self-interest and focus on short-term, opportunistic exchange relationships, in which the individual actors can preserve their independence and high flexibility [12].

Vertical integration is considered to be the *make* (inside the company) decision, which means that a company integrates a successive stage, which can be an upstream or a downstream process. Hence, vertical integration combines different levels of the value chain within one firm [11]. Internal, intra-firm transactions replace various market transactions. This can be achieved either by forming a subsidiary or by a merger or acquisition. In vertically integrated firms, management directives dictate the transfer of resources across stages [2].

The classic *make* vs. *buy* decision has been researched quite well. Based on Coase's work about boundaries of a firm that make the difference whether companies choose to *make* or *buy* the product [13], Williamson [14] was one of the first to speak about hybrid governance structures. Based on the previous research made on the topic of hybrid coordination strategies and hybrid governance structures, Peterson et al. have highlighted the hybrid strategies and the nature of the so-called vertical coordination continuum. Depending on the type of vertical transaction, firms decide between the spot market, vertical coordination (productive partnerships) and vertical integration [12, 15]. Vertical integration combines different levels of the value chain within one firm [11]. Internal, intra-firm transactions replace various market transactions. This can be achieved either by forming a subsidiary or by a merger or acquisition. In vertically integrated firms, management directives dictate the transfer of resources across stages [2].

Vertical coordination can be described as the synchronisation of successive stages in the marketing channel from producers to consumers, leaving out spot market transactions, where the commodity exchange is only based on pricing. Productive partnerships, a kind of vertical integration, are characterised by collaborations of independent firms, in which the partners share interests as well as knowledge and resources to improve the outcomes of the supply chain activity. Productive partnerships can be based on specification contracts (production and marketing contracts[2]), relational-based alliances and equity-based alliances [12]. It can take different organisational forms possible: from loose or tacit agreements to stable, long-term and trust-based cooperation contracts [14, 17].

One can assume that the higher the priority to secure quality and/or quantity of raw materials, the stronger is the shift from spot market transactions towards advanced vertical coordination mechanisms [18]. This is closely related to the intensity of control, which increases along the continuum (**Figure 1**). With spot markets, the intensity of control is low, as exchange partners decide on whether to realise the transaction or not. With specification contracts, the control increases from that related to spot markets. As in relation-based alliances, involved firms share risks and benefits; coordination control arises from mutual interests and decision-making. In equity-based alliances, the intensity of control is even higher, because partners are key stakeholders and control and decision-making are decentralised among the ownership parties. Examples for equity-based alliances are cooperatives and joint ventures [12, 15].

### 2.2 Contracting in productive partnerships

The key for all types of vertical coordination is contracting. Vertical coordination aims to overcome the disruptions in supply and inferior-quality products. However, the key actors (retailers and processors) find themselves constrained not

[2] For an overview on different classifications of agricultural contracts, see Drescher [16].

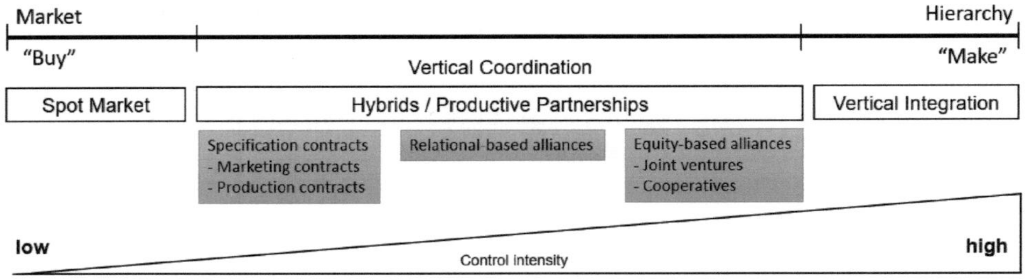


**Figure 1.**
*Framework vertical coordination (based upon [12]).*

by their capital capacity but by that of other participants along the chains on which they depend for critical inputs. This is because traditional lending institutions such as banks do not give credit to enhance the inter-firm product flow. Contract farming can be defined as an agreement between legally independent firms for the production of a commodity or product for a future market [16]. Götz et al. state: "An essential element of contract farming is the provision of some degree of assistance to the farmers, with the aim of increasing supply quantity or quality, or reducing seasonality" ([19], p. 364). Overall, farm assistance can include input supply programmes, investment assistance, trade credits, bank loan guarantees, extension and management advisory services, etc [4]. Thus, farm assistance programmes must be accompanied by appropriate governance mechanisms.

Production contracts (resource-providing contracts) are predominantly used to address quality concerns [20]. Developed markets have various consumer segments with differentiated demands. In production contracts, the contractor provides, on the one hand, a market for the goods and, on the other hand, engages in many of the producer's decisions and retains ownership of essential production inputs to secure higher-quality products to attend to the differentiated demands of the consumer segments [21]. However, when the higher-quality products become standardised (e.g. IFS or GlobalGAP certified) and there are no supply difficulties and/or the overall product quality is not complex, mainly marketing contracts will be used.

Marketing contracts address only the issue of supply disruptions by private contractual initiatives [22, 23]. The contractor usually provides a market for the goods but—on the contrary to production contracts—engages in few or none of the producer's decisions. In marketing contracts, the contractor and producer may negotiate the delivery schedule, pricing method and product characteristics.

For both types of contracts, Swinnen states that "these private contract initiatives can be quite substantial" ([2], p. 1). Empirical evidence indicates that they include farm management assistance, extension services, quality controls, farm input assistance programmes, trade credits and even bank loan guarantees. The programmes generate essential improvements in the credit situation of the farms, as they contribute directly to improved access to finance (e.g. through trade credit) and indirectly as they improve contracting farms' access to loans from banks or external financial institutions (through loan guarantees, enhanced farm profitability and improved future cash flows). Summing up, there are different factors influencing participants towards contract arrangements.

The main reason why processors enter into contracts includes the control over input supply. Further, processors use contracts to achieve uniformity and predictability to suit consumers, but they also benefit from lower costs in processing, packing and grading [24–27].

The main motivating factors for farmers to enter into contracts are the following, as reported by the USDA (1996): (I) income stability (to reduce risk compared to other ways of selling on traditional marketing channels); (II) improved efficiency (management decisions are transferred to the farmers); (III) market security (entering the contract provides a certain security in that the product will be sold if it meets with the requirements); and (IV) access to capital (contractor often provides inputs for farmers, which reduces the usage of credits) [28].

However, two reasons for the breaching of contracts have been detected. First, a lack of trust in business relations between producers and their buyers, as in transition countries, many buyers experienced that businesses were not able to pay. According to Ring and Van de Ven, trust is not built based on contracts; it rather emerges over time due to the commitment of assets or satisfactory performance [29].

Second, they may not be able to fulfil a contract because they cannot access basic production factors [23]. Contract enforcement is still an important problem. In the World Bank study, the enforcement problem was regarded as one of the most important barriers for successful vertical coordination [4]. However, in some cases, public enforcement institutions are not fully functioning. Furthermore, since transition countries are often described as having limited social capital, there is also an absence of societal enforcement mechanisms (e.g. peer or community pressure, a sense of mutual obligation and an overall sense of distrust). Thus, to improve the farmer's access to basic production factors (capital and specific inputs) and know-how/information (knowledge and experience), means have to be worked out and put down in writing, i.e., contracts have to be signed [4].

The change to modern procurement systems is one reason for initiating vertical coordination and, therefore, chain-based financing. The requirements set by these systems favour large-scale farm production for two purposes: (1) significantly fewer large suppliers are needed, and hence the complexity of the system is lowered, which decreases transaction costs, and (2) it is more costly to assist small farms than larger farms [4]. As a result, many retailers and processors would like to see growth in farm size.

However, retailers and processors are (still) forced to include smallholders. Smallholders are essential for ensuring the required quantities in some countries. Particularly in labour-intensive sectors, small-scale farming has significant cost

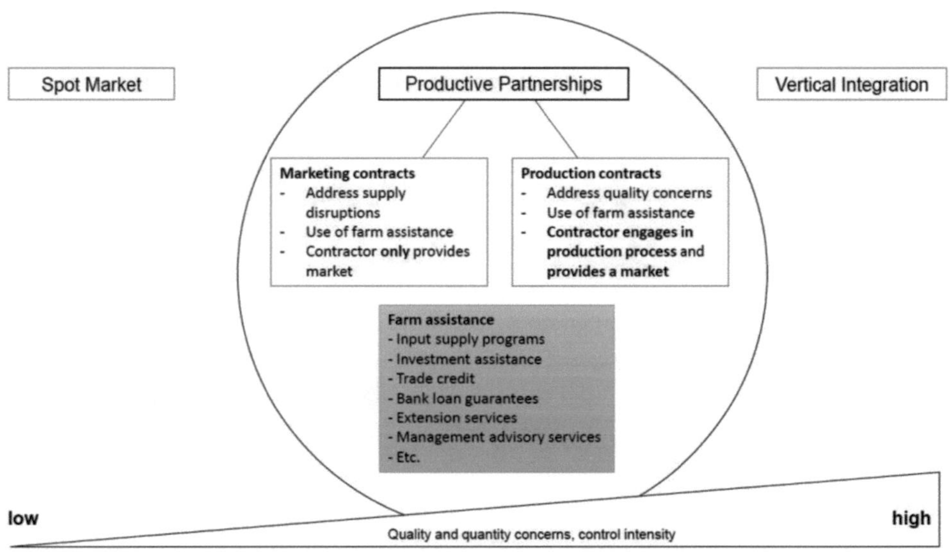


**Figure 2.**
*Contracting in productive partnerships.*

advantages. If the (farm) suppliers get too large, they begin to recapture some power. Since larger farms have the feeling that they can survive just by themselves, it may be more likely that smaller farmers join horizontal collaborations and ultimately create much larger units. The degree of market development is essential for the degree of vertical coordination. The less a market and its institutional environment are developed, the less likely it is that a complex system of vertical coordination will emerge (where marketing contracts are dominant). The more developed a market (i.e. the greater the demand for higher-quality products), the higher the degree of vertical coordination will be, and production contracts are favoured. These contracts vary in control allocation and risk transformation across stages.

**Figure 2** sums up the elements of contracting in productive partnerships.

## 3. Background information: Armenian wine industry

During the communist era, the satellite countries were divided to focus on the production of particular products. Therefore, Armenian table wine production was shifted mainly to brandy production, which led to a significant change in the Armenian wine culture. Other countries, such as Georgia and Moldova, were focusing on wine production, which preserved the wine culture within these countries [30].

The production area has gone through a tremendous decline after a very peak in 1985 with 35,000 ha (~88.4 million litres). During the Soviet times, Armenia processed more than 200,000 tons of grapes mostly for brandy, a little bit of wine and sparkling wine. The major part of the production was consumed in Russia and the empire of the Soviet Union. Especially the anti-alcohol campaign in 1985 initiated by Michail Gorbatschow had an enormous influence on the area until the collapse of the Soviet Union in 1991 [31]. His goal was to improve the Soviet morale, to reduce the expenses and deaths due to high alcohol consumption. Many old vineyards were cut off or removed to reduce the production of alcoholic beverages [32]. **Figure 3** gives an overview of the wine production from 1971 to 2017.

In the post-Soviet period, the grape-growing industry declined heavily in Armenia and other Soviet countries, and so did the wine sector due to changes in

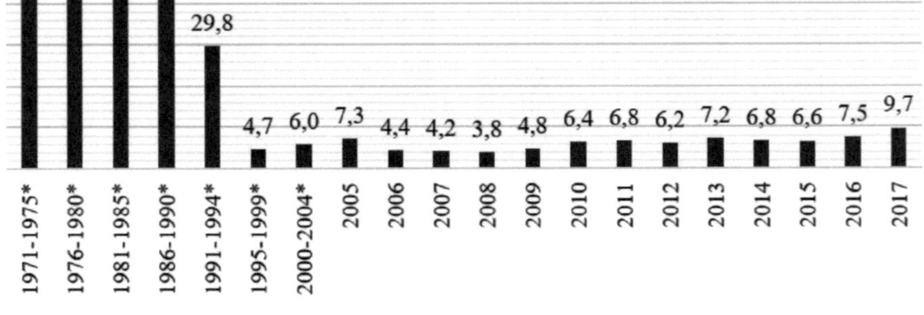


**Figure 3.**
*Wine production (incl. base wine for brandy) in million litres in Armenia from 1971 to 2017 annually (based upon [33, 34]).*

land privatisation. Other influencing factors were the absence of replantation of vineyards and the shift of some farmers to other more profitable crops [1]. Triggered by the lack of productivity, outdated machinery and issues in bulk purchasing systems, problems of adaption to new emerging markets occurred. All these issues led to a drastic rise in terms of vine cultivation costs [31, 35]. Some producers terminated their production ultimately or shifted to new industries. Since the early 1990s (with an interruption due to the financial crisis), the grape-growing sector slowly has recovered in terms of production numbers, mainly because of an upswing in the brandy sector.

For brandy production, mainly white grape varieties, which can deliver higher yields and sugar levels (to obtain higher alcohol content for brandy making), are cultivated. Those varieties are less suitable for table wine production. Red varieties are mostly used for table wine production, where, in addition to sugar level, healthiness and other quality aspects such as ripeness, acidity and pH level are more important. Therefore, prices between red and white grapes are tremendously different—white grapes receive overall lower payments [1].

Producers purchase mostly grapes from small rural households with small average sizes of grape-growing units leaving the grape growers in a weak spot for bargaining. According to Hanf et al., most of the grape-buying agreements (besides YBC contracts) in the wine and brandy industry are based on quantity and trust [10]. They do not include quality criteria. Currently, informal, 1-year oral agreements are usually closed before harvest, but mostly repetitive during the years. The case of not observed contracts was also found in Armenia and has led to mistrust [10].

In 2017, overall, 66,544 farmers cultivated grapes in an average plot size of 0.23 ha [36]. Due to their plot sizes, many smallholders cannot manage to finance their winemaking facilities and/or get access to the market to sell the high-valued final product. That is why farmers are heavily dependent on their grape sales to a few operating production plants such as wineries or brandy factories [1]. The dependence on grape sale for smallholders is still high, as it is the primary source of rural income.

## 4. The case study: Yerevan brandy company

The YBC is (still) the leading brandy-producing enterprise of Armenia. Currently, the YBC has around 2500 private farmers delivering grapes to the company on a contract basis. It produces a range of brandies of different ages. The brand Ararat belongs to the company. The YBC exports up to 90% of the production to 33 countries worldwide. The primary export destination is Russia. The company comprises four production sites, in three grapes are received, the juice is fermented, and the interim product (wine) is distilled. In all four sites, the distillate is aged. The fourth site is in Yerevan, where the ageing, blending and bottling facilities as well as other divisions such as HR, IT, accountancy and administration are situated. The YBC has branches in Ararat, Armavir and Tavush.

To gain insights into the production structures, operational procedures and business relationship to the smallholders which supply grapes to the company, a qualitative research approach was chosen. Qualitative research is dedicated to a limited number of cases that are investigated as precisely as possible. Therefore, face-to-face individual interviews were conducted with different industry participants. Besides representatives of the company itself, we interviewed smallholders (grape producers) and industry experts from politics and education as well as experts from foreign help organisations, e.g. Deutsche Gesellschaft für Internationale Zusammenarbeit (GIZ), Center for Agribusiness and Rural Development (CARD), Centre for the Promotion of Imports (CBI) from developing countries, etc. Additionally, we interviewed the director of the Vine and Wine Foundation of Armenia, who represents all grape growers and processors in the industry. Regarding the company's perspective, we interviewed the heads of grape purchasing and quality control at the YBC and two of the YBC agronomists, who work directly together with the farmers in the vineyards. Moreover, we conducted interviews with 15 smallholders who have a contract with the company. To cover all production sites of the YBC, we have interviewed five farmers from each region. Some of the farmers have worked with the YBC for many years, and others have just recently started the collaboration. Interviews are based on a semi-structured interview guideline and were carried out by the authors personally. The interviews took place between May 2018 and January 2020. The interviews were conducted in Armenian and then translated into English to guarantee full exploitation of information.

For the qualitative analysis of the interviews, the approach of Gläser and Laudel [37] was used. They use a method called extractive qualitative content analysis. It is based on a structuring technique to extract relevant and complex information during the whole process. The process is completely open for new and unexpected information. After the information is extracted from the original text material (transcribed interviews), the information is processed and analysed.

The case study of the YBC shows how an international company manages to integrate local smallholders (grape growers) into their national and international value chains by using means of vertical coordination in the form of contracting. Moreover, the case study demonstrates how a procurement system can be installed successfully in a weak institutional setting. The YBC was the first company in Armenia to introduce the contracting system between the grape growers and processors in 2003. Later it was recognised by the government as an exemplary one.

After the Yerevan Brandy Company became part of the Pernod Ricard Group in 1998, an internal restructuring process has taken place to tackle the issues of the brandy industry and to align them with the international standards of the markets. Main changes were carried out in infrastructure, refurbishment, huge investments specifically in winemaking facilities and distilleries were made, but the most important changes were made in business management. The introduction of the first written, enforceable and long-term contracts changed the standards of the wine and brandy industry in Armenia.

The main reason why the YBC entered into contracting was to ensure sustainable grape supply in terms of quantity. To secure the needed quantity, the company has to purchase all their grapes from independent grape growers, as the YBC does not possess a large area of own vineyards except for 0.5 ha of trial vineyard. The company is forced to include smallholders to ensure the required quantity.

The contract, which is set up between the company and the grape growers, contains specifically the grape quantity, variety, contract length, characteristics of the plot where the grapes are grown and a few quality criteria such as the healthiness of the grapes and the minimum sugar level. One interviewed grape grower mentioned, for instance: "It is required to deliver healthy grapes. The delivered quantity should contain the smallest possible amount of material other than grapes (e.g. leaves, stones). The contract also includes the grape varieties which can be delivered to the company". The guaranteed quantity enables grape growers to plan in terms of income, input supplies and production. Through the long-lasting approach (3–5 years of contracting), trust is built between both parties. As one interview partner said: "For me it's not only the profit that matters. Most important is the long-term collaboration with the YBC, as it gives me a feeling of stability".

The interviewed farmers stated that the duration of the long-term contracts in the past was even 7 years.

Furthermore, the contract includes terms of payments and delivery (e.g. number and time of payments). All types of contracts include minimal prices. The company philosophy aims to purchase grapes at a price above the farmer's production cost, which is company-wide evaluated before harvest.

In general, the price is announced in spring, which gives farmers the possibility to decide what to do. However, in some exceptional years (e.g. 2018) pricing details can vary, so the YBC announces the updated price before the harvest. As prices are included in the contracts and the contracts are legally enforceable, neither the farmer nor the YBC can negotiate on prices after the contract has been set up.

An annex of the contract takes into account the potential deviation from the contractual agreements due to quantity fluctuations. In August, shortly before the harvest starts, the YBC agronomists visit the vineyards and calculate the potential yield. If weather conditions were unfavourable and the farmer could not obtain the required quantity (or, in turn, the yield is higher than expected), the agronomists and farmers can fix the required quantity according to the situation. A grape grower stated: "The yield is always predicted by the agronomists beforehand. Depending on year the quantities can be higher or lower, but it is negotiable by the contract annex".

Ten agronomists are working at the YBC doing quality control within the contracted vineyards to provide consultancy to the farmers. One of the farmers, for instance, said: "There was a time we were implementing old cultivation methods damaging our crop. In the beginning it was difficult to change our mind-set and follow the instructions of the YBC agronomists. Time proved the effectiveness of their consultancy so we became more open to their suggestions, even more motivated to find out new information, learn new cultivation technologies". The consultancy includes good agricultural practices such as pruning, canopy management, spraying times with herbicides/pesticides, greenings, etc. Additionally, the agronomists also conduct monitoring to make sure that the expected grape quality and yield are going to be received. Based on the evaluation of the agronomists, the company subsidises smallholders with farm input assistance—if needed—with pesticides, herbicides and fertilisers. Another grape grower mentioned: "The company provides tools, sprayers, and pesticides at convenient prices. The payment for these inputs is directly taken out from the pay-out we receive for the delivered grapes".

To provide knowledge and new techniques, the YBC owns 0.5 ha of experimental plots for trials. For instance, in 2006 the company started some trials on their experimental plots together with the Pernod Ricard research centre, to demonstrate their grape suppliers that new cultivation methods in the grape production can be less time-consuming and more profitable.

For smallholders, the main motivating factors to enter into contracts with the YBC are based on the benefits the farmers receive from working with the company. The YBC provides constant market access for grapes and gives the smallholders a guarantee of grape purchase. Farmers who do not breach the contract have a stable, reliable and almost predictable profit/income. The long-term relationship between the company and the farmers offers the opportunity to build trust between the contracting parties. This increases reliability between them and gives income security to the farmers. Besides some 1-year contracts, mostly 3–5 years of contract length (if there is no contract breach), are used. Another advantage is that grape delivery and payments are scheduled ahead; hence, no price negotiations of the YBC are possible if the farmer meets the contract requirement due to legal enforcement. The company provides farm assistance in the form of inputs (chemicals, fertilisers, etc.) and consultancy (pruning, irrigation, spraying times, dosage and frequency, etc.), if necessary. Farmers have access to knowledge and new techniques through the YBC. Grape producers also benefit from working with the YBC because they are delivering high-quality grapes for high-quality brandy production and thus benefit of the company's reputation.

One of the smallholders, for example, said as a concluding remark: "My father and I were practicing grape cultivation ever since land privatisation in Armenia. We had a small plot and low quantities. Slowly, gaining experience in this field, our expectations rose, and at the same time, the vineyard territories expanded, especially in the period when PR bought the YBC and we started collaboration. The organizational skills of the company positively surprised us from the very beginning. It was the first time in Armenia, when the farmer delivers the grapes without being stuck in huge queue. Everything was planned with a contract".

If it comes to the credit situation of the smallholders, the YBC is not helping them directly by providing loans, loan guarantees or trade credits. However, smallholders who work with the YBC over a longer period increase their chances to get a credit or loan at external institutions because of the fixed, long-term contracts with the YBC and, hence, a stable and enhanced profitability or improved future cash flows based on their past performances. This provides security to external institutions, improving the probability for smallholders to finance investments. One statement of an interviewed grape grower was: "Having larger vineyards, one always needs financial support to do investments in, for example, the trellising system (metal wires, etc.). Recently I expanded my vineyard and needed a bank loan. When applying for the loan the bank considers your current economic situation as well as where you are trading your product. Seeing our contract with a serious company such as the YBC, the bank never rejects the application". In this setting, the YBC helps indirectly with access to capital.

In case a farmer cannot deliver the settled quality and/or quantity of grapes to the YBC, the contract is breached. Additionally, the competition among smallholders to work with the YBC is huge, creating societal pressure to follow the restrictions.

The contract design, as mentioned above, shows that the YBC is on the one hand working with marketing contracts to secure grape quantities and qualities for their brandy production. In general, the brandy production itself does not require highly differentiated grapes. Grape quality is mainly defined by a minimum sugar level and a minimum of the healthiness of grapes close to the harvest. However, the YBC sets up higher-quality restrictions. For instance, the company only purchases high-level healthy grapes (pest-free, disease-free, no foreign bodies, etc.) and certain grape varieties. The YBC does not purchase all grape varieties which can be used for brandy production.

In contrast to that, grape production for wine is more differentiated, and quality is also defined by sugar and healthiness, but it includes further grape characteristics such as colour, tannins and sugar and acid ratios. However, if we consider on the other hand the provided farm input assistance in the form of chemicals, fertilisers, etc. and the consultancy, e.g., pruning, irrigation and spraying times, this depicts a high involvement during the production process. The YBC actively engages in many critical decisions within the production process, adding production contract features.

Further interviews with some producers of table wine and experts from related fields such as education, politics and related fields/companies were conducted additionally. The interviews revealed that after the successful implementation of contracts in the brandy sector, many table wine producers followed. One of the experts stated: "Most of the time grape purchases for table wine were based on customary rearrangements. In that area a very well developed relationship, only one company has. This is Yerevan Brandy Company, having written contracts with their

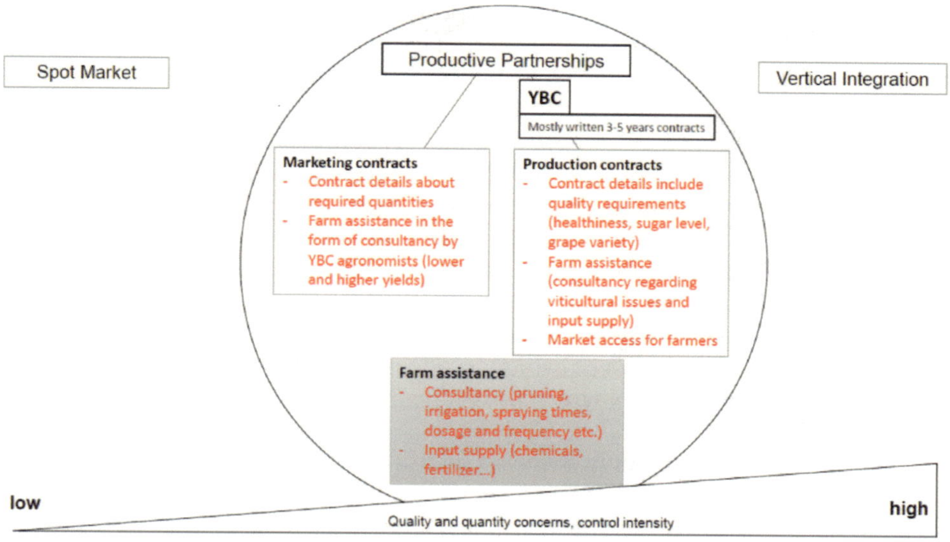


**Figure 4.**
*Results of vertical coordination in the YBC case study.*

farmers. In this sense, Yerevan Brandy was a role model". Another expert added that within the last years, a steady increase in contracts in the grape purchase was notable. Overall, the influence of the YBC in the brandy and wine sector of Armenia was shown.

**Figure 4** sums up the results of vertical coordination mechanisms used in the productive partnerships of the YBC and the grape growers.

## 5. Conclusion

As a result of land privatisation which was part of the transition process, the average plot sizes of farmers are small. In 2017, overall, 66,544 farmers cultivated grapes in an average plot size of 0.23 ha. Due to their plot sizes, many smallholders cannot manage to finance their winemaking facilities and/or get access to the market to sell the high-valued final product, resulting in a high dependency of smallholders on grape sales to processors. In this context, the aim was to show how to integrate smallholders into national and international value chains by successfully installing a procurement system in weak institutional environments. In our case study of the Yerevan Brandy Company, we found that the company uses specification contracts as one type of vertical coordination, where independent individuals or firms of different stages in the value chain decide to collaborate. Currently, the YBC has around 2500 private farmers delivering grapes to the company on a contract basis. In order to avoid the disruptions in supply and inferior quality, the company introduced contracting from the early beginning. As a result, major disruptions in quantity and quality never occurred.

In 1998, Pernod Ricard Group bought the Yerevan Brandy Company, the most important Armenian brandy-producing company known by its Ararat brandy. This was when the first contracts between producers and smallholders were introduced. The YBC serves as a role model for other post-Soviet countries with similar issues up to the present.

Introducing the contracting system Yerevan Brandy Company reached a synchronisation of successive stages in the vertical marketing channel from producers to consumers to overcome problems of supply and quality. The YBC is taking different measures regarding vertical coordination. For example, the company uses mostly 3- to 5-year contracts, which include specifications of the grape quantity, variety, contract length, characteristics of the plot where the grapes are grown and a few quality criteria such as the healthiness of the grapes and the minimum sugar level. This shows that the YBC uses production contracts rather than pure marketing contracts. The company also offers farm assistance in the form of consultancy of YBC agronomists who closely work together with the farmers in the vineyards and in the form of input supply. Agronomists provide consultancy for viticultural practices, special viticultural issues, measures to take if yields are lower or higher than expected and input supply. The example of the YBC also shows that foreign direct investment not only brings capital, production facilities and technology transfers but also creates employment, provokes new job skills and offers management expertise.

The business environment in Armenia should embrace and reduce the obstacles for foreign companies to make investments in Armenia. This opens the opportunity for domestic producers to benefit financially, knowledge- and technology-wise, access to export markets as well as in business management from foreign direct investments.

In addition, the legal framework has to be improved to guarantee the enforcement of contracts and oral agreements. Especially grape growers, who are in a weak bargaining spot, would benefit from a legal improvement. Furthermore, NGOs or the ministry of agriculture could provide contract templates to reduce the numbers of oral agreements, as the legal setting for written contracts is more developed and enforcement exists.

The study finds that the institutional arrangements used in Armenia in the form of contract farming as part of vertical coordination are beneficial for both the processing company and the smallholders. In these contracts, the farmers agree to produce and supply agreed quantities of grapes. The study could not find any disadvantage for smallholders in terms of contract farming. In contrast, farmers who have a contract with the YBC benefit of secured market access, secured and stable income, access to bank loans, education, farm assistance in the form of consultancy or input supply.

For farmers who are not working with the YBC, a general recommendation is a higher financial support from the government or other institutions, which would help to ease their situation. The financial support in forms of credits or loans enables the grape growers to invest into more demanded varieties (e.g. red grapes for table winemaking) or even into other crops (e.g. lemons, peaches) which are more profitable.

Another option to support smallholders is the establishment of cooperatives. Cooperatives are beneficial for smallholders, as the bundling of quantities improves their bargain situation and knowledge—as well as investment—sharing is possible. The delivered grapes can be divided into quality categories, which then can be sold in different price segments to different market participants. The offer of differentiated quality levels with different prices leads to higher overall profits. Farmers who produce high-quality grapes gain higher patronage, giving an incentive for high-quality production. If wine or brandy producers need grapes or wine, they can bargain with the cooperative as a single entity for their needed quality category, and they do not have to bargain with many farmers to gain the same quantity.

All in all, the YBC manages to integrate smallholders (grape growers) into their national and international value chains by successfully installing a procurement system by using different measures of vertical coordination. Additionally, the YBC contributed to the development of the sector. Other companies start to adapt and take the YBC as a role model. In future, the standards set by the YBC and the ongoing development (education, knowledge, experience, etc.) will improve the performance of many farmers and equalise the produced qualities on the market. Sugar levels, healthiness of the grapes and usage of certain grape varieties become basic quality requirements. When the higher-quality products become standardised (e.g. IFS or GlobalGAP certified), mainly marketing contracts will be used. Thus, in the long run, it can be assumed that the degree of vertical coordination will decrease and the contracts will further tend towards pure marketing contracts. However, in the short and medium term, the adjustment will assumingly be rather slow.

## Author details

Linda Bitsch[1], Silva Atoyan[2], Barbara Richter[1*], Jon Hanf[1] and Taras Gagalyuk[3]

1 Hochschule Geisenheim University, Geisenheim, Germany

2 Armenian National Agrarian University, Yerevan, Armenia

3 Leibniz Institute of Agricultural Development in Transition Economies (IAMO), Halle (Saale), Germany

*Address all correspondence to: barbara.richter@hs-gm.de

## References

[1] Bitsch L. A structural analysis of the Armenian Wine Industry: Elaboration of strategies for the domestic market [thesis]. Giessen: Justus-Liebig-Universität / Hochschule Geisenheim University. Yerevan: Deutsche Gesellschaft für Internationale Zusammenarbeit (GIZ) GmbH; 2017

[2] Swinnen JFM, When the Market Comes to You – Or Not; The Dynamics of Vertical Coordination in Agri-Food Chains in Transition. Final report on "Dynamics of Vertical Coordination in ECA Agri-Food Chains: Implications for Policy and Bank Operations". The World Bank; 2005

[3] Buchenrieder G, Hanf JH, Pieniadz A. 20 years of transition in the agri-food sector. German Journal of Agricultural Economics. 2009;**58**(670-2016-45783):285-293

[4] van Berkum S. Restructuring and vertical coordination in the dairy sector in Romania. In: Swinnen JFM, editor. Case Studies: The Dynamics of Vertical Coordination in Agrifood Chains in Eastern Europe and Central Asia. Washington, DC: World Bank; 2005. pp. 167-189

[5] Blomström M, Sjöholm F. Technology transfer and spillovers: Does local participation with multinationals matter? European Economic Review. 1999;**43**:915-923

[6] Borensztein E, De Gregorio J, Lee JW. How does foreign direct investment affect economic growth? Journal of International Economics. 1998;**45**:115-135

[7] Barrell R, Holland D. Foreign direct investment and enterprise restructuring in Central Europe. The Economics of Transition. 2000;**82**:477-504

[8] Bevan AA, Estrin S. The determinants of foreign direct investment into European transition economies. Journal of Comparative Economics. 2004;**32**:775-787

[9] Dyker DA. Technology exchange and the foreign business sector in Russia. Research Policy. 2001;**30**:851-868

[10] Hanf JH, Marquardt V, Urutyan V, Babayan A. The impact of foreign direct investment on the agribusiness of transition countries: The example of the Armenian wine business. International Journal of Business and Globalisation. 2016;**16**(4):423-447

[11] Hanf JH, Gagalyuk T. Integration of small farmers into value chains: Evidence from Eastern Europe and Central Asia. In: Egilmez G, editor. Agricultural Value Chain. London: IntechOpen Ltd.; 2018

[12] Peterson HC, Wysocki A, Harsh SB. Strategic choice along the vertical coordination continuum. International Food and Agribusiness Management Review. 2001;**4**(2):149-166

[13] Coase RH. The nature of the firm. Economica. 1937;**4**(16):386-405

[14] Williamson OE. Markets and Hierarchies: Analysis and Antitrust Implications. New York, NY: Free press; 1975

[15] Martinez SW. Vertical Coordination of Marketing Systems: Lessons from the Poultry, Egg, and Pork Industries. USDA, AER: ERS; 2002. p. 807

[16] Drescher K. Assessing aspects of agricultural contracts: An application to German agriculture. Agribusiness: An International Journal. 2000;**16**(4):385-398

[17] World Bank. Rural Finance Innovations: Topics and Case Studies, Report No. 32726-GLB,

The World Bank, Agriculture And Rural Development Department; 2005

[18] Hanf JH. Processor driven integration of small-scale farmers into value chains in Eastern Europe and Central Asia. In: Tanic S, editor. Enhancing Efficiency and Inclusiveness of Agri-Food Chains in Eastern Europe and Central Asia. Budapest: FAO Regional Office for Europe and Central Asia; 2015. pp. 13-36

[19] Götz L, Njavro M, Hanf JH, Pieniadz A. Vertical coordination with growers in the supermarket fresh fruit and vegetables supply chain in Croatia. German Journal of Agricultural Economics. 2009;**58**(670-2016-45660):363-370

[20] Gorton M, White J, Chernyshova S, Skripnik A, Vinichenko T, Dumitrasco M, et al. The reconfiguration of post-soviet food industries: Evidence from Ukraine and Moldova. Agribusiness: An International Journal. 2003;**19**:409-423

[21] Martinez SW, Reed A. Vertical Coordination by Food Firms Rising Along with Contract Production, Report AIB-720. Washington, DC: Economic Research Service/USDA; 1996

[22] Dries L, Swinnen JFM. Globalisation, quality management and vertical coordination in food chains of transition countries. In: Proceedings of the 92nd EAAE seminar on Quality Management and Quality Assurance in Food Chains. Göttingen; 2-4 March 2006

[23] Gow HR, Swinnen JFM. Up- and downstream restructuring, foreign direct investment, and hold-up problems in agricultural transition. European Review of Agricultural Economics. 1998;**25**:331-350

[24] Boland M, Barton D, Domine M. Economic Issues with Vertical Coordination. Ames, IA: Agricultural Marketing Resource Center; 2002

[25] Drabenstott M. Consolidation in U.S. agriculture: The new rural landscape and public policy. Economic Review. 1999;**84**:63-71

[26] Sykuta M, Parcell J. Contract structure and design in identity-preserved soybean production. Review of Agricultural Economics. 2003;**25**(2):332-350

[27] Tsoulouhas T, Vukina T. Integrator contracts with many agents and bankruptcy. American Journal of Agricultural Economics. 1999;**81**:61-74

[28] USDA. Farmers' Use of Marketing and Production Contracts, Report No. 747. Washington, DC: Farm Business Economics Branch of the U.S. Department of Agriculture, Rural Economy Division, Economic Research Service; 1996

[29] Ring P, Van de Ven A. Developmental processes of cooperative interorganizational relationships. Academy of Management Review. 1994;**19**:90-118

[30] Bitsch L, Ghvanidze S, Hanf JH. "Die Wiege des Weinbaus" - weinwirtschaftliche Entwicklung im Kaukasus. In: Deutsches Weinbau Jahrbuch. Vol. 70. Stuttgart: Ulmer; 2019. pp. 144-149

[31] Johnson H, Robinson J. The World Atlas of Wine. 7th ed. London: Mitchell Beazley; 2013. p. 45

[32] Scannell NJ, Newton JG, Ohanian R. Viticulture, wine production, and agriculture in armenia. Economic sectors in transition. JABR. 2002;**18**:4. DOI: 10.19030/jabr.v18i4.2125

[33] NSS National Statistical Committee of the Republic of Armenia. Statistical

Yearbook of Armenia. Yerevan: State Council on Statistics; 2001-2016

[34] Harutyunyan A. Viticulture and Winemaking in Armenia. Yerevan: Written in Armenian; 2007

[35] Gasparyan S. Report of a working group on Vitis: First meeting. In: Maul E, Eiras Dias JE, Kaserer H, Lacombe T, Ortiz JM, Schneider A, et al., editors. European Cooperative Programme for Plant Genetic Resources ECPGR. Pálic, Serbia and Montenegro; 2003

[36] Urutyan V. Assessment of Management Systems of Wineries in Armenia. In: International Wine Conference Yerevan; 2017. Available from: https://icare.am/wp-content/uploads/2017/11/VWFA_Conference_Urutyan-2.pdf [Accessed: 08 April 2018]

[37] Gläser J, Laudel G. Experteninterviews und qualitative Inhaltsanalyse als Instrumente rekonstruierender Untersuchungen. 4th ed. VS-Verlag: Wiesbaden; 2010

Section 2

# Reviews of Agricultural Issues

Chapter 5

# Factors Affecting Efficiency of Vegetable Production in Nigeria: A Review

*Iyabo Bosede Adeoye*


## Abstract

Vegetables are important for maintenance of good health; their production and marketing are veritable sources of employment and livelihood. To promote vegetables' contribution to the above, there is a need for sustainable and efficient production process. The paper reviewed production, socioeconomic factors, and constraint affecting efficiency of production of three important vegetables (tomato, pepper, and onion). The review showed that socioeconomic factors found to increase technical efficiency in vegetable production were educational level, extension contact, and household size. Influence of farmer age on technical efficiency was inconclusive due to varied opinions. Increase in farm size, quantity of seed, amount of fertilizer, and agrochemical were found to have positive influence on output. Majority of the literature reviewed opined that increase in quantity of labour raises productivity; however, it must be utilized efficiently. The mean technical efficiency of the vegetables varied from the southern to the northern part of the country. The cross cutting constraints in vegetables production are pest and diseases, inadequate storage facilities, and high cost of improved inputs. The study recommends increase awareness and sensitization on optimum levels of resource use for increased productivity and appropriate intervention to constraints in the value chain.


**Keywords:** vegetables, productivity, socioeconomic factors, production inputs, Nigeria

## 1. Introduction

Vegetable is one of the important sources of vitamins and minerals [1] and dietary fiber [2] and are essential in prevention of diseases [3]. Vegetable production is of great economic importance in the agricultural sector [4]. Its value chain can provide income and reduces poverty and unemployment [1]. Vegetable production has the potential to increase food security and create employment [5]. Smallholders' farmers made up large number of vegetable producers in Nigeria [6].

Insufficient intake of fruit and vegetables is estimated to cause around 14% of gastrointestinal cancer deaths, about 11% of ischemic heart disease deaths and about 9% of stroke deaths [7]. The World Health Organization recommended consumption of 400 g of fruits and vegetables daily to maintain good health. Vegetables production is profitable, and the actors will require adequate knowledge, capital, and new methods [8].

Tomato, pepper, and onion are important vegetables in the global economy due to their high consumption [1]. Tomato is one of the foremost, essential vegetables in Nigeria [9], virtually consumed by every tribe [10], and grown all over Nigeria [11]. Tomato stands out as one of the important vegetables considering the scale of production and level of consumption [12]. It is beneficial for the maintenance of good health and disease prevention [13]. Tomato production presents an opportunity for increasing rural incomes particularly among peri-urban smallholder farmers due to the high demand in urban centers [14]. Farmers are willing to cultivate tomato more than any other vegetable because of its high demand, multiple harvests produced [15]. Tomato is produced across Nigeria and smallholder farmers cultivating between 0.5 and 4 hectares of land account for 90% of production [16]. Tomato is mainly produced by resource poor small farmers with small farm holdings and they are responsible for the tomato consumed in the nation [17].

Tomato production is profitable in Nigeria, and average profit of tomato production under irrigation was N128,750 ($ = N350) in Kogi and Benue State [18], while the rate of naira on naira invested on tomato production in Kano was 1.5 indicating profitability of the enterprise [19].

Pepper is a rich source of vitamins A, C, and E [20]. It is a high value crop [21] and has economic significance in the world market. It has potentials to generate foreign exchange and can be utilized in confectionary, medicinal, and culinary purpose [22]. Pepper production is an important source of foreign exchange and its exportation in Nigeria has been reported to be lucrative [23]. The northern part of Nigeria is the major areas of production [20, 22], and it is mostly produced by smallholder farmers [24].

Onion is an important vegetable and is of commercial importance throughout the world [25]. Onion production in Nigeria is profitable with rate of returns on investment of 91.89 and 119.78% in Sokoto and Kebbi state [26]. Onion consumption and demand is throughout the year [27]. Onion is used as spice, vegetable, salad, and dressing [28]. The production of onion can improve economic status and welfare of farmers [29]. In Nigeria, bulk of onion is produced under irrigation in the Northern states [30].

Despite the importance of vegetable in the daily diet and the competitive and comparative advantage the country has in the production, vegetable production is fluctuating [6]. For instance, the average yield of tomato is far below the potential of the crop. For instance, the average yield of about of 6 tones is much lower than 7 tones and 6.48 tones reported for Tanzania and Uganda, respectively [31]. Agricultural production can be sustained through efficient resource use [32]. Efficiency is the ability to produce maximum output from the least input combination during the production process [33, 34]. Efficiency is crucial in resource saving [35]. Factors influencing efficiency of farmers can be categorized into agent and structural facts [36]. Agents' factors are educational level, age, and social capital, while structural factors include farm size, fertility, and among other [37].

Analyzing efficiency levels provides understanding of constituent of efficiency system and strategies to improve efficiency [38]. It is worthy of note that efficient utilization of resources leads to improvement in production [38]. Improvement in technical efficiency of farmers will lead to better yield, food security, and better standards of living [39].

A series of studies have been carried out to assess and compiled factors affecting agricultural productivity and its drivers in Nigeria, which include [40–44]. They have focused on commodities such as rice, maize, and tuber crops. None of the aforementioned studies, however, has compiled factors affecting efficiency of vegetable production in Nigeria. This paper intends to identify and collate factors affecting efficiency of vegetable production in Nigeria.

## 2. Methodology

The study made use of literature on efficiency of vegetable production in Nigeria from. Studies from the different geopolitical zones of Nigeria were collected and reviewed to identify the production inputs and socioeconomic factors reported to have influence on vegetable production in the country. Primary data and stochastic frontier production model were employed by majority of the reviewed literature.

### 2.1 Factors affecting efficiency of tomato production

#### *2.1.1 Age*

Age is one of the important determinants of agricultural production because age of farmers may affect adoption of agricultural innovations. Older farmers were more technically efficient compared to younger farmers in tomato production at Kwara and Adamawa states, Nigeria [45, 46]. Contrarily, an increase in farmer's age was found to increase technical inefficiency in tomato production in Benue State [11]. In other countries in Africa, older farmers are more technically efficient than their younger counterparts in Cameroon and Swaziland [39, 47]. They attributed this to their respective years of experience in the production of the commodity. Succinctly, the impact of age on technical efficiency of tomato production is inconclusive due to the various outcomes of the impact on tomato production.

#### *2.1.2 Education*

Number of years spent in school was found to be positively and significantly related to the output of tomato farmers [11, 48]. Educated households were exposed to information and able to manage farm production better [49]. The higher the level of education, the more enlightened a farmer becomes in adopting new innovation with its multiplier effect on increased output. According to [39] in Cameroon, on tomato production, higher level of education of farmers results in increasing technical efficiency of farmers. This is justifiable as new techniques, and innovations are introduced daily especially with the presence of research institutions. Households that are educated will adopt such novel techniques and technologies and increase their technical efficiency. Presumably due to their enhanced ability to acquire technical knowledge, which makes them move close to the frontier output. Since most authors confirmed positive effect of education on technical efficiency, the factor can be adjudged to improve productivity.

#### *2.1.3 Household size*

Household size had a positive and significant effect on technical efficiency of tomato production in Oyo state [50]. This indicates that efficiency increases with increase in household size. Increase in household size improved tomato production in Benue and Adamawa States [11, 46]. Households with large family size may serve as a readily available source of labor. Thus, it can be inferred that household members may be a ready source of labor in farming activities.

#### *2.1.4 Extension contact*

Increase in extension contact increases the output from tomato production [48]. This is expected as extension agents have been known for their role in smallholder production. According to a study in Cameroon on tomato production, the nearer a farmer is to an extension agent, the higher will be his technical efficiency [39]. The extension provides latest information on production techniques, provision of information on improved seeds, and provision of agronomic knowledge. The farmer can avail himself of all the above to boast his productivity and technical efficiency.

#### *2.1.5 Farm size*

An increase in the hectares of farm land put into tomato production will lead to an increase in the output of tomato [10, 48]. Increase in farm size will lead to increased output of tomato and that land is a very important factor in tomato production [11, 31, 46, 51]. Additionally, in Cameroon, increase in area put into tomato production leads to increase in yield of the commodity [39]. Thus, increase in area of land put into tomato production may lead to increase in output of tomato.

#### *2.1.6 Labor*

Increase in the quantity of labor had been found to increase the output of tomato in Benue and Kano State, Nigeria [10, 48]. Furthermore, increase in the labor lead to improvement in tomato output in Kaduna and Kwara states [31, 45]. Thus, adequate number of labor at the appropriate time may lead to increase in the output of tomato. Although care must be taken not to over use labor, thus optimum level must be adhered to in order not to lead to reduction in the returns due to overutilization of the input.

#### *2.1.7 Seed quantity*

A unit increases in the level of seed lead to increase in tomato output [31]. Increase in seed quantity was found to lead to increase in tomato output [10, 11, 22, 31, 51]. Increase in quantity of seed positively influences tomato output in Cameroon [39]. A 1% increase in seed under tomato production will raise the output of tomato production; thus, seed is a very important factor of production [46].

#### *2.1.8 Chemical (such as fertilizer and insecticides)*

An increase in the level of chemical and organic fertilizer will lead to increase in tomato output [31]. Increase in pesticides use will lead to increased output of tomato [11]. Increase in the quantity of herbicide and fertilizer lead to increase in tomato output [51].

Increase in the quantity of fertilizer lead to improvement in tomato output [10, 11, 31] This is expected because nonfertile soil will not support good growth and development of the commodity. It is very important to note that optimum level of the above resources must be utilized. This is very important in relation to herbicides, pesticides, and fertilizer because when they are overused, they may have adverse effect on the health of the consumers.

### 2.2 Factors affecting efficiency of pepper production

#### *2.2.1 Age*

Increase in age of farmers increases technical inefficiency indicating that older farmers are less efficient in pepper production [20, 52]. This may be due to the fact that older farmers may not be agile to search for new information that may lead to improvement in pepper production. Older farmers were also found to be technically inefficient in pepper production in Ethiopia [53]. Additionally, increase in the number of years of farmer's experience reduces technical inefficiency [52, 54]. This may indicate that experience gathered over time in the production of the commodity may be put into use to improve practices in the production. This showed that there are various opinions on the effect of age on technical efficiency of pepper farmers.

#### *2.2.2 Household size*

In a study on pepper production in Ogun state, increase in household size may lead to increase in efficiency of pepper production [20]. This may be due to increase in number of individuals that may assist in farm operations.

#### *2.2.3 Extension contact and member of cooperative society*

Increase in extension contact was also found to increase technical efficiency [20, 53]. This may be attributable to the fact that extension agent will be able to build capacity of producers on improved method of production and disseminate information on improved practices to the farmers. The reviewed literature also indicated that being a member of cooperative society may lead to increase in efficiency in pepper production [54]. This may be due to the fact that the members of the society will be able to pull resource together and share knowledge that may lead to increase in productivity.

#### *2.2.4 Education*

Education was also found to have positive effect on efficiency of pepper farmers [20, 52, 54]. Educated farmers will be able to adopt innovations in production which may be necessary to improve yield. In Ethiopia, farmers that were educated were more technically efficient in pepper production compared to those with no education [53].

#### *2.2.5 Farm size, seed quantity, and fertilizer*

Increase in farm size was found to lead to increase in quantity of pepper produced [52–54]. Additionally, seed quantity was found to increase quantity of output. Thus, increase in the quantity of seed [55] may lead to increase in efficiency and output of pepper. Increase in quantity of fertilizer was found to increase output of pepper [52, 55]. This is expected because nonfertile soil may lead to low productivity.

#### *2.2.6 Labor*

Increase in the quantity of labor will lead to increase in output of pepper [55]. This may be due to the fact that pepper production may be labor intensive but over utilization of the resources should be prevented in order not to lead to decline in output.

### **2.3 Factors affecting efficiency of onion production**

#### *2.3.1 Farm size*

Increase in the size of land put into onion production may increase output of the commodity [30, 56]. Thus, output may be increased by putting more land into production. It was also discovered that putting more land into onion production may increase output of the commodity in Ethiopia [57].

### 2.3.2 Chemicals

Increase in the quantity of fertilizer and agrochemical such as herbicides was also found to increase output of onion [30, 57]. This is expected because low soil fertility will reduce productivity.

### 2.3.3 Labor

Increase in labor lead to increase in onion output [56]. Labor quantity must be optimum in order not to lead to reduction in the output of onion [30].

### 2.3.4 Education

Increase in education level of farmers was found to have positive influence on technical efficiency, thus increase in education level may bring about increase in the efficiency of farmers [30]. Educated farmers may be able to carry out the practices in order to improve the output of the commodity. Increase in farming experience, household size, and extension contact was also found to increase technical efficiency [30] (**Table 1**).

| Commodity | Factors | Study area | Authors | Effect of factor on productivity |
|---|---|---|---|---|
| Tomato | Age/farming experience | Northcentral (Benue state) | Abur [11] | Factor has inconclusive effect on productivity |
| | | Northcentral (Kwara) | Adenuga et al. [45] | |
| | | Northeast (Adamawa) | Zalkuw et al. [46] | |
| | Education | Northcentral | Abur [11] | Factor increases productivity |
| | | | Ibitoye et al. [48] | |
| | | Cameroon | Tabe-Ojong and Molua [39] | |
| | Extension contact | Northcentral | Ibitoye et al. [48] | Factor increases productivity |
| | | Cameroon | Tabe-Ojong and Molua [39] | |
| | Household size | Northcentral | Abur [11] | Factor increases productivity |
| | | Southwest | Ogunniyi and Oladejo [50] | |
| | | Northeast (Adamawa) | Zalkuw et al. [46] | |
| | Access to Credit | Northcentral | Adenuga et al. [5] | Factor increases productivity |
| | Farm size | Northeast | Tijjani et al. [51] | Factor increases productivity |

| Commodity | Factors | Study area | Authors | Effect of factor on productivity |
|---|---|---|---|---|
| | | Northcentral | Abur [11] | |
| | | Northcentral | Ibitoye et al. [48] | |
| | | | Saleh et al. [10] | |
| | | Northwest | Umar and Abdulkadir [31] | |
| | | Northeast (Adamawa) | Zalkuw et al. [46] | |
| | | North central | Adenuga et al. [45] | |
| | Seed quantity | Northeast | Tijjani et al. [51] | Factor increases productivity |
| | | Northcentral | Abur [11] | |
| | | | Saleh et al. [10] | |
| | | Northwest | Umar and Abdulkadir [31] | |
| | | Northeast (Adamawa) | Zalkuw et al. [46] | |
| | | Northcentral | Adenuga et al. [45] | |
| | Labour | Northcentral | Abur [11] | Factor increases productivity |
| | | Northwest | Umar and Abdulkadir [31] | |
| | | Northcentral | Adenuga et al. [45] | |
| | Chemicals such as herbicide and fertilizers | Northeast | Tijjani et al. [51] | Factor increases productivity |
| | | Northcentral | Abur [11] | |
| | | | Saleh et al. [10] | |
| | | Northwest | Umar and Abdulkadir [31] | |
| | | Northcentral | Adenuga et al. [45] | |
| Pepper | Age/farming experience | Southwest | Dipeolu and Akinbode [20] | Factor effect on productivity inconclusive |
| | | Southeast | Ugwu [52] | |
| | | Northwest | Mohammed [54] | |
| | | Northwest | Adeoye et al. [55] | |
| | Household size | Southwest | Dipeolu and Akinbode [20] | Factor increases productivity |
| | | Southeast | Ugwu [52] | |
| | Extension contact | Southwest | Dipeolu and Akinbode [20] | Factor increases productivity |

| Commodity | Factors | Study area | Authors | Effect of factor on productivity |
|---|---|---|---|---|
| | | Northwest | Mohammed [54] | |
| | Education | Southeast | Ugwu [52] | Factor increases productivity |
| | | Northwest | Mohammed [54] | |
| | Farm size | Southeast | Ugwu [52] | Factor increases productivity |
| | | Northwest | Mohammed [54] | |
| | Seed quantity | Northwest | Mohammed [54] | Factor increases productivity |
| | | Northwest | Adeoye et al. [22] | |
| | Fertilizer | Northwest | Adeoye et al. [22] | Factor increases productivity |
| | Labor | Northwest | Adeoye et al. [22] | Factor increases productivity but must be utilized efficiently. |
| | | Southeast | Ugwu [52] | |
| Onion | Farm size | Northwest | Ojo et al. [30] | Factor increases productivity |
| | | Northeast | Grema and Gashua [56] | |
| | Fertilizer | Northwest | Ojo et al. [30] | Factor increases productivity |
| | | Northeast | Grema and Gashua [56] | |
| | Labor | Northwest | Ojo et al. [30] | Factor effect on productivity inconclusive |
| | | Northeast | Grema and Gashua [56] | |
| | Education | Northwest | Ojo et al. [30] | Factor increases productivity |
| | Extension contact | Northwest | Ojo et al. [30] | Factor increases productivity |
| | Household size | Northwest | Ojo et al. [30] | Factor increases productivity |

**Table 1.**
*Summary of factors affecting efficiency of vegetable production.*

## 3. Mean technical efficiency of vegetable production

Mean technical efficiency of tomato production in Benue state was 0.59 [11], Kwara 0.78 [45], and Adamawa (0.68) [46]. The mean technical efficiency of pepper production in Enugu state was 0.70 [52] indicating that there is still capacity to improve on the present efficiency level. The technical efficiency of pepper of 0.90

| Commodity | Location | Author | Mean technical efficiency |
|---|---|---|---|
| Tomato | Northcentral | Abur [11] | 0.59 |
| | Northcentral | Adenuga et al. [45] | 0.78 |
| | Northeast | Zalkuw et al. [46] | 0.68 |
| Pepper | Southeast | Ugwu [52] | 0.70 |
| | Northwest | Mohammed [54] | 0.90 |
| Onion | North | Ojo et al. [30] | 0.95 |
| | Northcentral | Ibrahim and Omotesho [58] | 0.92 |

**Table 2.**
*Summary of mean technical efficiency of vegetables.*

was obtained in Kaduna state [54]. Mean technical efficiency of onion according in the northern state of Nigeria was 0.947 [30]. Mean technical efficiency of 0.92 was obtained for onion in north central Nigeria [58] (**Table 2**).

## 4. Constraints to vegetable production

The major constraints to tomato production are pest and diseases [9, 10, 19]. Major constraints in pepper production were price fluctuation, activities of middlemen, and high cost of inputs such as fertilizer, labor, and seeds [54]. Other problems were pests and diseases infestation in the field. The producers may experience price fluctuation most especially in the peak period of production especially when there are no processing facilities. Activities of middlemen may disrupt income that may be realized by the farmers in the production process.

Constraints in onion production include high cost of production input, lack of storage facilities, limited access to improved seeds, pests, and diseases, and lack of effective extension services [56].

## 5. Conclusion and recommendations

The review revealed that educational status, household size, and extension contact are important factors influencing producers' efficiency in tomato production. Production inputs such as seed and chemicals such as fertilizers are critical to increased yield of tomato. Although increase in the quantity of labor may raise productivity, it must however be utilized efficiently. The study recommends sensitization and increased awareness on optimum level of resource use for increased tomato production in order to improve contribution of the commodity to economic empowerment.

## Author details

Iyabo Bosede Adeoye
National Horticultural Research Institute, Ibadan, Nigeria

*Address all correspondence to: bosedeadeoye2005@gmail.com; iyabs1@gmail.com

## References

[1] Schreinemachers P, Simmons EB, Wopereis MCS. Tapping the economic and nutritional power of vegetables. Global Food Security. 2018;**16**:36-45

[2] Ulger TG, Songurn S, Grak O, Cakiroglu FP. Role of Vegetables in Human Nutrition and Disease. London, UK: Intech Open; 2018. pp. 7-32. DOI: 10.5772/intechopen.77038

[3] Xaba BG, Masuku MB. Factors affecting the productivity and profitability of vegetables production in Swaziland. Journal of Agricultural Studies. 2013;**1**(2):37-52

[4] Stoeva T. Factors affecting the vegetable farming efficiency in Bulgaria. Scientific Papers Series "Management, Economic Engineering in Agriculture and Rural Development". 2012;**12**(4):30-32

[5] Smith FI, Eyzayuirre P. African leafy vegetables: Their role in the World Health Organization's global fruit and vegetable initiative. African Journal of Food, Agriculture, Nutrition and Development. 2007;**7**(3):1-17

[6] Ogunbo MM, Ayinde IA, Afolami CA, TOA B. Technical efficiency of pepper production under tropical conditions. International Journal of Vegetable Science. 2015;**21**(1):21-27

[7] WHO. Promoting fruit and vegetable consumption around the world. 2020. Available from: https://www.who.int/dietphysicalactivity/fruit/en/index2.html

[8] Dias JS. World importance, marketing and trading of vegetables. Acta Horticulturae. 2010;**921**:XXVIII

[9] Aboki EI, Umaru I, Mshelia SI, Luka P. Resource use efficiency of irrigated tomato production in northern part of Taraba state, Nigeria. International Journal of Agriculture Innovations and Research. 2014;**3**(2):512-515

[10] Saleh RA, Kajidu YB, Abubakar IM. Resource use efficiency in tomato production in a semi-arid zone of Nigeria. International Journal of Trend in Research and Development. 2016;**3**(3):554-558

[11] Abur CC. An assessment of irrigated tomato farming on resource productivity of farmers in Vandeikya local government area of Benue state: Application of technical efficiency model. Global Journal of Human-Social Science. 2014;**14**(1):43-50

[12] Adejobi AO, Babatunde RO, Idowu EO. Weight and measurement issues in retail marketing of fresh tomatoes: Evidence from Osun state. The Journal of Agricultural Science. 2011;**6**(4):20-26

[13] Usman J, Bakari UM. Profitability of dry season tomato (*Lysipersicom esculentum Mill*) production in Fufore local government area of Adamawa state, Nigeria. International Journal of Engineering Science. 2013;**2**(11):113-117

[14] Takesure T. Factors influencing commercialization of smallholder tomato production case of Domboshava, Goromonzi, District in Zimbabwe. A thesis submitted in partial requirement of degree of Master of Science in Agriculture and Applied Economics to the Department of Agriculture and Extension, Faculty of Agriculture, University of Zimbabwe; 2017

[15] Hanadi EA, Mohammed IM, Salih EE. Value chain analysis for tomato production and marketing in Khartoum state, Sudan. Current Investigations in Agriculture and Current Research. 2018;**5**(4):651-657

[16] Sahel Newsletter. The Tomato Value Chain in Nigeria. 2017;**15**:1-8. Available from: http://sahelcp.com/wp-content/uploads/2017/07/Sahel-Newsletter-Volume-15.Tomato.pdf

[17] Adenegan KO, Adeoye IB. Price analysis of tomato in rural and urban retail markets of Oyo state. Journal of Agricultural Economics and Rural Development. 2011;**4**(2):90-96

[18] Ayoola JB. Comparative analysis of tomato under irrigation and rainfed systems in selected local government areas of Kogi and Benue state, Nigeria. Journal of Development and Agricultural Economics. 2014;**6**(11):466-471

[19] Katanga YN, Danwawu SS, Musa B. Economic analysis of tomato production in Fagge local government, Kano state, Nigeria. Journal of Economics and Development Studies. 2018;**6**(2):98-104

[20] Dipeolu AO, Akinbode SO. Technical, economic and allocative efficiencies of pepper production in Southwest Nigeria: A stochastic frontier approach. Journal of Agricultural Economics and Rural Development. 2008;**17**(1):24-33

[21] Aliyu L, Yahaya RA, Arunah UL, Haruna IM. Response of two chilli pepper varieties (*Capsicum frutescens* L.) to harvesting frequency. Elixir International Journal. 2012;**42**(2012):6493-6495

[22] Mohammed B, Abdulsalam Z, Ahmed B. Profitability in Chilli pepper production in Kaduna state, Nigeria. British Journal of Applied Science & Technology. 2016;**12**(3):1-9

[23] Ajibefun IA, Daramola AG. Determinants of technical and allocative efficiency of micro–enterprises: Firm–level evidence from Nigeria. African Development Bank. 2003;**4**:353-395

[24] Hay J. Pepper, peppers, hot peppers, agriculture and capsaicin. Facts and Details. 2009. Available from: http://factsanddetails.com/world/cat54/sub345/item1609.html

[25] Abdu Z, Abba A, Chigoze AS, Mohammed AB. Resource use efficiency in onion production among participating and non-participating farmers in Hadejua Valley, irrigation project, Jigawa state Nigeria. Journal of Agriculture and Veterinary Sciences. 2015;**8**(8):69-73

[26] Dogondaji SD, Bala KM, Mohammed I. Profitability and resource use efficiency in dry season onion production in Sokoto and Kebbi state, Nigeria. International Journal of Agricultureand Rural Development. 2007;**9**(1):35-39

[27] Obasi IO, Kalu ON. Structure and efficiency of onion market in Umuahia area of Abia state, Nigeria. International Journal of Economic and Business Management. 2019;**5**(1):40-47

[28] Baree MA. Measuring technical efficiency of onion farms in Bangladesh. Bangladesh Journal of Agricultural Research. 2012;**37**(1):171-178

[29] Hussaini MA, Amans EB, Ramalan AA. Yield, bulb size distribution and storability of onion (Allium cepa) under different levels of N fertilization and irrigation regime. Tropical Agriculture. 2000;**77**(3):145-149

[30] Ojo MA, Mohammed US, Adeniji B, Ojo AO. Profitability and technical efficiency in irrigated onion production under middle Rima Valley irrigation project in Goronyo, Sokoto state Nigeria. Continental Journal of Agricultural Science. 2009;**3**:7-14

[31] Umar ASS, Abdulkadir MB. Analysis of resource-use efficiency and productivity of residual soil moisture

tomato production in Kaduna state, Nigeria. International Letters of Social and Humanistic Sciences. 2015;**51**:152-157

[32] Udoh EJ. Land management and resource use efficiency among farmers in South – Eastern Nigeria [unpublished PhD thesis]. Ibadan, Nigeria: Department of Agricultural Economics, University of Ibadan; 2000

[33] Musaba E, Bwacha I. Technical efficiency of small scale maize production in Masaiti district, Zambia: A stochastic frontier approach. Journal of Economics and Sustainable Development. 2014;**5**(4):104-111

[34] Anang BT, Stefan B, Sipiläinen T. Agricultural microcredit and technical efficiency: The case of smallholder rice farmers in northern Ghana. Journal of Agriculture and Rural Development in the Tropics and Subtropics. 2016;**117**:189-202

[35] Sanusi RA, Ashaolu OF, Akogun CO, Ayinde AFO. Effect of poverty on production efficiency of vegetable farming households in Ogun state, Nigeria. Nigerian Journal of Agricultural Economics. 2015;**6**(1):65-80

[36] Van Passel S, Mathijs E, Nevens F, Huylenbroeck GV. Measuring farm sustainability and explaining differences in sustainable efficiency. Ecological Economics. 2007;**62**(1):149-161

[37] Ogada MJ, Mwabu G, Ngui D, Mathenge M. Technical efficiency of Kenya's smallholder food crop farmers: Do environmental factors matter? Environment, Development and Sustainability. 2014;**16**(5):1065-1076

[38] Najjuma E, Kavoi MM, Mbeche R. Assessment of technical efficiency of open field tomato production In Kiambu County, Kenya (stochastic frontier approach). Jomo Kenyatta of Agriculture and Technology Journals. 2016;**17**(2):21-39

[39] Tabe-Ojong MP, Molua EL. Technical efficiency of smallholder tomato production in semi-urban farms in Cameroon: A stochastic frontier production approach. Journal of Management and Sustainability. 2007;**7**(4):27-35

[40] Adebayo EF. Resource use efficiency and multiple production objectives of dairy pastoralists in Adamawa state, Nigeria [unpublished PhD thesis]. University of Ibadan; 2006

[41] Adeoti AI. Economic analysis of irrigation and rainfed production systems in Kwara state, Nigeria [unpublished PhD thesis]. Department of Agricultural Economics, University of Ibadan; 2002

[42] Awotide OD. Resource use efficiency and inputs institutions in upland rice production in Ogun State, Nigeria [unpublished PhD thesis]. Department of Agricultural Economics, University of Ibadan; 2004

[43] Ogundele OO, Okoruwa VO. A comparative analysis of technical efficiency between traditional and improved rice variety farmers in Nigeria. African Journal of Economic Policy. 2006;**11**(1):91-108

[44] Rahji MAY. An analysis of the production efficiency of broiler firms in Ibadan area of Oyo state Nigeria. Tropical Animal Science Journal. 2003;**6**(2):103-109

[45] Adenuga AH, Muhammad-Lawal A, Rotimi OA. Economics and technical efficiency of dry season tomato production in selected areas in Kwara state, Nigeria. Agris On-line Papers in Economics and Informatics. 2013;**5**(1):11-19

[46] Zalkuw J, Singh R, Pardhi R, Gangwar A. Analysis of technical

efficiency of tomato production in Adamawa state, Nigeria. International Journal of Agriculture Environment & Biotechnology. 2014;**7**(3):645-650

[47] Malinga NG, Masuku MB, Raufu MO. Comparative analysis of technical efficiencies of smallholder vegetable farmers with and without credit access in Swazil and the case of the Hhohho region. International Journal of Sustainable Agricultural Research. 2015;**2**(4):133-145. DOI: 10.18488/journal.70/2015.2.4/70.4.133.145

[48] Ibitoye SJ, Shaibu UM, Omole B. Analysis of resource use efficiency in tomato (*Solanum lycopersicum)* production in Kogi state, Nigeria, Asian. Asian Journal of Agricultural Extension, Economics & Sociology. 2015;**6**(4):220-229

[49] Abebe G. Off-farm income and technical efficiency of smallholder farmers in Ethiopia: A stochastic frontier analysis [Master thesis]. SLU; 2014. p. 662

[50] Ogunniyi LT, Oladejo JA. Technical efficiency of tomato production in Oyo state, Nigeria. Agricultural Science Research Journal. 2011;**1**(4):84-91

[51] Tijjani MS, Goni M, Bukar AU. Analysis of resource-use efficiency in tomato production in jere, Borno state, Nigeria. Journal of Biology, Agriculture and Healthcare. 2018;**8**(18):1-4

[52] Ugwu SI. Technical efficiency in the production of Nsukka yellow pepper among rural farmers in Enugu North, agricultural zone, Enugu state, Nigeria, dissertation submitted to the Department of Agricultural Economics in the Partial Fulfillment of the Requirement for the Award of Master of Science (M.Sc) degree in Agricultural Economics, University of Nigeria, Nsukka; 2010

[53] Kibret BG, Abebo MT. Technical efficiency of red pepper production and its determinants among smallholder farmers in Shashogo district of Hadiya zone, SNNP region, Ethiopia. Journal of Resources Development and Management. 2019;**58**:43-52

[54] Mohammed B. Analysis of resource use efficiency and profitability in chilli pepper (*Capsicum frutescens*) production and its contribution to household farm income in Kaduna state [unpublished thesis]. Zaria: Department of Agricultural Economics, Ahmadu Bello University; 2015

[55] Adeoye IB, Fashogbon AE, Idris BA. Analysis of technical efficiency of pepper production among farmers under tropical conditions. Journal of Vegetable Science. 2014;**20**(2):124-130

[56] Grema IJ, Gashua AG. Economic analysis of onion production along river Komadug area of Yobe state, Nigeria. Journal of Agriculture and Veterinary Sciences. 2014;**7**(10):5-11

[57] Abdul Kadir KO. An evaluation of the efficiency of onion producing farmers in irrigated agriculture: Empirical evidence from Kobo District Amhara region, Ethiopia. International Journal of Agricultural Extension and Rural Development. 2015;**2**(5):116-124

[58] Ibrahim HY, Omotesho OA. Determinant of technical efficiency in vegetable production under Fadama in northern Guinea savannah, Nigeria. International Journal of Agricultural Technology. 2013;**9**(6):1367-1379

Chapter 6

# Basics of Good Business Plan for Small-Scale Agribusiness Investors in Nigeria

*Mustapha Momoh, Caroline Aturu-Aghedo and Nana Usman Bature*

## Abstract

This chapter provides a synthesis of planning small-scale entrepreneurial skills to guide the current and prospective micro investors to harness wide ranges of agribusiness value chains in Nigeria. This initiative considered alternatives in business strategic options to harness the potentials therein, which involve production, distribution, processing of agricultural products and services integration for converting agricultural outputs for regular and timely supply of domestic and international needs. The current outcry for economic diversification couple with high rate of unemployment in Nigeria requires concerted efforts to boost the agriculture sector as a viable alternative for growth and development. Suffices to say, most agribusiness investors more often than not, experience failure because of the dearth of requisite business skills for planning the survival and growth of small-scale agribusinesses in the face of modern realities. In this wise, the chapter brings the benefits such as risk mitigation, cost savings, and income generation through combination of known production planning and business management skills. The chapter adopts discursive taxonomy, interpolating elicited facts from available literature plus the knowledge of 'on-the-job-experience' to promote and support the development of agribusinesses strategy for the transformation of the agriculture sector to generate employment, income, and promote food security, and competitiveness in the marketplaces.

**Keywords:** good business plan, micro investors, agribusinesses, management skills, diversification

## 1. Introduction

The motivation and commitment to develop this write-up for planning micro investment in agribusiness value-chains emanates from rational observations and conviction. On the foremost, the youths' colossal neglects of agriculture business versus very high unemployment rates and the consequential poverty and misery in the country, for me, are unacceptable. More, so, this scenario is worsen by the population explosion demanding for food and the influx of imported food into the country, which further overstretched the country's balance of payment crises. Another observable and convincing scenario is the under developed agricultural food processing systems in Nigeria deserving cogent attention. Traditionally, the country produce primary crops like cocoa, cotton, tomatoes, grains, ginger, etc., but imports beverages, textile materials, canned tomatoes, malt-drinks, ginger drinks, etc. imposing unbalance trade of payments leading to constant devaluation of our currency, which has to stop. Furthermore, the perceived very high potentials of agribusinesses in Nigeria and, under tapped agro-industry value-chains in many states of Nigeria calls for strategic attention and investment. Indeed, the availability of management skills could be very much helpful in order to arrest these ugly trends by adding value to agricultural products thus, boost rural incomes, reduce youth restiveness, boost GDP and improve balance of payment deficit in the long-run.

The objectives of the paper is to give readers, policy makers, micro agribusiness investors, farmers and local government administrators a clear understanding of the following:

- Meaning of small-scale agribusiness
- Classification of small-scale agribusiness
- The nature and scope of small business in Nigeria
- A good business plan
- Importance of good business plan
- Preparing a good business plan
- Features of a good feasibility study
- Writing a good business plan

## 2. Meaning of small-scale agribusiness

A business is a concern, an enterprise, or organisation set up by an individual or group of individuals for making profits from operations of the concern. According to [1], a business is an initiative, which involves the production of goods and services to meet up consumers' need and satisfaction. Agribusiness ventures in Nigeria comprises of micro, small and medium to large productive units. Indeed, the description of what small agribusiness means varies from one country to another. It also differs from one industry to another, where each country tends to derive her definition with understanding of the role agribusinesses perform in the growth and development of the country. More so, definitions of micro agribusiness do change overtime with respect to price levels, levels of technology and other considerations. Indeed, small agribusinesses are synonymous with small- and medium-scale enterprises (SMEs) in the context of this paper. In most developed countries, SMEs are usually referred to as small businesses.

On this note, a small agribusiness is an agricultural enterprise owned and operated privately with a small number of employees and relatively low volume of sales and income. Small agribusinesses are business concerns with a total capital investment not more than 2 million (₦2, 000, 000) and the number of employees not more than 50 [1].

## 3. Classification of small-scale agribusinesses

The methods used to classify small agribusinesses include but not limited to number of employees, annual sales and/or turnover, value of assets and net profit (balance sheet). According to [2, 3], small agribusiness classification differs amongst countries. For instance, in Australia, the Australian Bureau of Statistics classifies small agribusinesses as those employing fewer than 20 persons. The Australian tax office uses average annual turnover of less than $1 million and net assets of less than $3 million as the criterion in this classification. In Canada, agribusinesses are small if it has less than 100 workers in manufacturing and in the service subsector less than 50 workers. Similarly, in UK, the classification of agribusinesses goes thus; it is micro, if the number of full-time workers is less than 10; small business if the full-time workers range from 10 to 49. More so, UK further classified agribusinesses as medium sized with the number of full-time workers ranges between 50 and 249. Lastly, agribusiness are considered large, if the number of full-time workers is 250 and above.

In Nigeria, the classification of agribusinesses takes dissimilar dimension. In addition to the classification based on the number of full-time workers, volume of assets is also considered. The volume of assets consideration however, excludes investment in landed properties in the classification. Notable classifications of the agribusinesses, according to [4] includes small agribusiness, which refers to enterprises with investment and working capital of 750,000 or less and the number of full-time employment stands at 50 workers or less. The medium-scale agribusinesses are enterprises that are functioning with investment and working capital within the range of over 750,000 and 3 million. However, the current inflation trend in the country put this classification in jeopardy, as these figures are unreliable. Hence, the National Council of Industry gave a more realistic classification, which includes:

- The micro and cottage industry relative to agribusinesses has a total investment and working capital of not more than ₦1.5 million; and, a labour size of not more than 10 workers and excluding landed properties.

- Small-scale agribusiness industry are businesses with a total capital of not more than ₦50 million including working capital, and, a labour size of not more than 100 workers minus cost of landed properties fits into the categorisation of 'small-scale agribusinesses'.

- Medium-scale agribusiness industry has a total investment and working capital of not more than ₦200 million including working capital, and a labour size of not more than 300 workers. This however excludes the cost of landed properties.

- Large-scale agribusiness industry includes businesses with a total investment and working capital of over ₦200million, and a labour size of over 300 workers minus cost of landed properties.

## 4. Nature and scope of small agribusiness

Small agribusiness activities in Nigeria found in these areas as identified by [2, 3] include:

- **Food processing enterprises**: food processing enterprises are the most common of small agribusinesses. This are commonly referred to as restaurant and fast-food businesses found everywhere serving the basic food needs of local and urban communities in both villages and towns. These agribusiness activities, more often than not, are owned and managed by women in the society.

- **Arts and craft**: Nigeria with many cultural traditions has a rich and diverse traditional arts and crafts heritage that many talented and gifted people engage in. Art and craft business is mostly found in urban settlements and the products are patronised by locals and international tourists.

- **Textiles and clothing**: this is one of the areas where agribusinesses are prominently practiced in Nigeria. The producers of textiles and clothing are small-scale enterprises found in commercial areas like Kano, Kaduna, Ibadan, Lagos, etc. This includes activities such as the tie-and-dye of textiles that prepares textile with different designs and colours to make them attractive. Moreover, the garment factory also helps to produce dresses of various shapes and types for local consumption. Over the years, textile industry in Nigeria has suffered poor commitments and foreign stringent competition. Indeed, stiff competition from technologically advanced foreign investors and products has led to closure of many title factories, drop in market share and loss of jobs and income.

- **Leather products**: Nigeria with its large livestock population of cattle, sheep, and goats, camel, and donkey has the raw material resources for thriving in the leather enterprises. The leather industries produce shoes, bags, decorative accessories, seat covers, furniture wears, etc. A typical example of leather enterprise is the Naraguta Leather Works in Jos, Plateau state, as well as in Kano and Sokoto states. Apart from the agribusinesses, small business activities in Nigeria are also found in building and construction enterprises, electronic and information technology ventures, basic metal and wood works, metal fabrication and engineering enterprises, amongst several others activities too numerus to mention that incorporate leather products in their finished outputs.

## 5. Samples of agribusinesses, practicable in Nigeria

This chapter also provides varieties of small agribusinesses that are commonly found and/or could be profitably practice in Nigerian soil:

i. **Crop production**: crop distribution and growth. Agronomic groupings of crops, crop culture (propagation, climate and soil requirements), fertilisers handling and distribution, and economic analysis of specific crops; maize, cassava, yam, rice, soya bean, cowpea, cotton, cocoa, citrus, oil palm, cashew, and vegetable. These depend on the cropping patterns and land use systems in the country.

ii. **Feed stuffs**: carbonaceous concentrates on grains, carbonaceous roughages, protein concentrates plant e.g. groundnut cola, soya bean meal, proteinases roughage's; commercial processing of feed stuffs: grinding, pelleting, etc. Feed standards and quality; nutrient requirements of various classes of livestock, chemical analysis such as proximate composition, anti-nutritional factors, feed microscopy and feed mills operations.

iii. **Animal production**: livestock production, breeds and breeding in farm animals. Management of different farm animal species, feeds and feeding, housing, handling and control, factors to be considered in establishing commercial livestock enterprises, disease management and control in farm animals.

iv. **Food processing technology**: post-harvest technology, modern techniques in food processing, packaging and storage, indigenous concepts and cottage industries for various food commodities.

v. **Fisheries production**: fish production in natural waters—rivers, lakes and in ponds. Management techniques for enhanced fisheries production in rivers, lakes, coastal waters and in ponds. Basic principles of fish culture; biotechnology in hatcheries and grow-cut operations; integrate fish farming, hatcheries and fish markets.

vi. **Forestry and wildlife investment**: tree plantation (dates, banana, mangoes etc.), economic cross breeding of plants such as India with local mangoes e.g. "Multala Iyako" breed (funnily refers as 'baba mai mangoro').

More so, [5] listed several small agribusiness enterprises, which intending small-scale investors could consider. They includes farmer's market vending, herb growing, vegetable farming, livestock feeds production, fruit packaging, nursery operation, dairy farming, poultry farming, fish farming, rabbit raising, snail farming, mushroom farming, beekeeping, honey production, beeswax processing, soy production, food delivery, and bulk foodstuff wholesaling. Others includes weed killer production, fruit canning, jam production, juice production, meat packing, hatchery operations, florist business, spice production, nut processing, organic gardening, sustainable farm consulting, agricultural equipment rental, worm farming, Christmas tree farming, firewood production, tree seed supply, oil production, potted plant sales, butterfly farming, wool production, pet food production, planting service, farm sitting, corn maze operation, petting zoo operation, agritourist/agro-tourism, lease hunting, and field crop farming. Explanatory note on 10 of these agribusiness options are as presented herewith:

i. **Herb growing**: this agricultural enterprise entails investing in herbs trees like basil, parsley and mint. Small-scale investors can grow them around their home and/or in field farm with great agriculture products, which provide raw materials to pharmaceutical firms within and outside the country.

ii. **Vegetable farming/food packaging**: small-scale investors can houseplant or plant it in garden a variety of vegetables which when harvested and sold in local market or preserved and transported to different urban markets, could generate lots of income. In fruit packaging, small-scale investors might not grow fruits directly but could deal in various types of fruit packaging for retail sells and/or make into other fruit based juices for commercial sales.

iii. **Dairy farming**: with the requisite skills and the ability to care for dairy animals such as cows, sheep and goats. Small-scale investors can easily engage in dairy farms where you produce milk, cheese and similar products in commercial quantity.

iv. **Fish farming**: fish farming is one the growing agribusinesses in Nigeria. Fish farming activities includes aquaculture, smoking, packaging, refrigeration, feeds production, wholesales and retailing.

v. **Rabbit rearing**: this is one of the emerging areas in animal-husbandry that has so far received negligible attention in Nigeria. The business is lucrative, easy to handle, weather friendly and not too risky. Rabbits can be raise for a variety of different purposes with meagre amount of money.

vi. **Snail farming**: snail farming is another emerging area in animal-husbandry in Nigeria that has also received negligible attention. The farming is as well very easy to handle with small amount of capital. Small-scale investors can raise snails for use as escargot and the slime has industrial usage for a variety of different purposes, thus, the business is very lucrative. However, it is not weather friendly and required secured environment. This attribute makes the business relatively risky.

vii. **Mushroom farming**: this is another emerging area in agribusiness venture in Nigeria that has also received negligible attention. The business is lucrative, easy to handle, weather friendly and not too risky. However, it grows best in a moist atmosphere. Small-scale investors can grow various types of mushrooms for domestic use as food supplements and medicinal usage. Mushroom is in high demand by pharmaceutical industry.

viii. **Beekeeping**: this agribusiness involves activities, which lead to a variety of different product-based business ventures such as honey production, wax production and crop pollination. Beekeeping requires high skills and start-up capital with little maintenance requirements.

ix. **Honey production**: for example, you can harvest honey from beehives and sell it to consumers or processors. Small-scale investors can produce honey for domestic use as food supplements and medicinal usage. Honey is in high demand by pharmaceutical industry too all over the world.

x. **Beeswax processing**: beeswax is one of the by-products of beekeeping that is lucrative and marketable in the global market. In other words, small-scale investors can take the advantage and venture into processing of beeswax for sale as raw material to individuals and companies that specialise in the production of candles and similar products.

The owner of any of the businesses listed above is refers to as an entrepreneur. S/he provides the capital required for the running of the business. S/he is the chief coordinator, controller and organiser of the agribusiness. Readers should learn the basis of agro-industrial value-chains and their environments explicitly, the technologies required as well as the emerging trends in technologies. It is of paramount importance to learn the skills for examining food industry, agribusiness systems, cost structure and sources of revenue in food industries. More so, the knowledge of international trade and agricultural policies, international monetary environment as it affects food and agro-allied industries, social and legal issues in the management of food and agro-allied industries are paramount. The knowledge of social and economic impact of food and agro-allied industries on the environment, developmental trends in food technologies and agro-allied industries is of great importance to small-scale agribusiness investors.

## 6. A business plan

A business plan means a formal written expression of outlined business goals. The definition also expresses the reasons why these goals are attainable and how to achieve them with the scope of available means. It contains background information about the enterprise and the entrepreneur. Thus, a good business-plan entails a clear statement of desired objectives, decision made and how to systematise and manage the scarce organisational resources to achieve the set objectives within a given period. More so, [6] gives the meaning of business plan as carefully refined thoughts and deliberate efforts a firm put in place from the onset towards achieving goals and/or the objectives. Indeed, the manner of utilising organisational resources gives the cardinal measure towards achieving profitability and/or other goals.

Hence, an agribusiness plan in the context of this paper revolves on four fundamental strategic questions, which includes 'what', 'how', 'where' and 'when' of the actions orientation in every business endeavour.

- **The 'What' question**: the question takes the form of 'what to produce', 'what to market', 'what to exchange', etc. this implies the needs for entrepreneurs to find suitable answers to such questions depending on the nature of the business. Whatever the entrepreneurs choose either to produce, market, exchange largely depends on the set objectives of the firm or enterprise. Therefore, an ideal agribusiness plan should state clearly, what line of action(s) the business endeavour to pursue in agricultural value chains.

- **The 'How' question**: this mode of question takes the form of 'how to produce', 'how to market', 'how to exchange', etc. it strategically involves the approach; process and/or technique require to achieve the set objectives of the business venture. Furthermore, the 'how' mode questions involves steps required to design specifically action-oriented programme of every business intent. On this note, therefore, it is expected of the entrepreneur to conduct total review of the business strategy and highlight the functional planning areas to help choose the appropriate method, process or technology for the effective execution of the plan. Small-scale agribusiness investors should take cognisance of the vital business components such as finance, market and human resources and production plans in providing answers to the how type question [6].

- **The 'Where' question**: this question mode takes the form of 'where to produce', 'where to market', 'where to exchange', etc. The 'where' question has to do with choosing the most appropriate business location. Indeed, it is very important to choose the most appropriate business location, bearing in mind strategic factors such as access to business information, raw materials, market, finance and skill labour in order to be prosperous.

- **The 'When' question**: similarly, the 'when' question mode takes the form of 'when to produce', 'when to market', 'when to exchange', etc. Indeed, every business endeavour is time bound. There should be a defined period to accomplish each step in the business schedule. A business plan without time bound is difficult to measure the progress overtime. It takes time to plan, execute, grow, develop and diversify. This true in every business venture of which agribusiness is not oblivious.

## 7. Importance of good business plan

A good business plan has the following importance:

- A good business plan adequately defines the vision and mission of the business. It identifies the key components of the goals, which eventually serves as implementation resume.

- Good business plan adequately allocate firm's available resources to handle foreseen and unforeseen challenges properly, in making crucial business decisions.
- A good business plan adequately provides information to all crucial segments of the business intent. The plan must as well inform the manager and/or all business actors on their roles, individually and collectively towards goals attainment.
- A good business plan vigorously pursues the most cost-effective processes that are easiest, fastest and cheapest to accomplish the set goals. This must be properly coordinated in an articulate manner to accomplish the set goal. Nevertheless, the easiest, fastest and cheapest as used in this context does not mean compromising standard. Indeed, operations standard must be maintained at all cost whilst pursuing the set goals of the firm.
- A good business plan bridges the gap from 'where we are' and 'what we have' to 'where we want to be' as well what we want to achieve. A journey of thousand miles start from zero (where we are), which progresses steadily to the destination (where we want to be).
- More so, a good business plan gives guidelines on the steps to be taking in a bid to achieve the target goals, whilst taking into account the realities of the available scarce resources. It must be well noted that every business is tied to the scope of available resources in order to achieve the desired goal(s).

## 8. Preparing a good business plan

In preparing a good business plan, it is crucial to find out whether or not (i) there exists viable market(s); or a new market platform can be created with easy for the product? (ii) How can the raw materials be obtained with ease? (iii) How can the skill labour be sourced with easy and at affordable cost? (iv) Is the necessary infrastructure readily available to facilitate operational activities? (v) The information on the costs of equipment, consumables and raw materials are known with absolute certainty. (vi) The sources of the expected income are known with absolute certainty, as well as been cost effective. (vii) There exists feasibility study report to guide the execution of the intended activities in the business plan.

Indeed, feasibility study report is the outcome of the preliminary investigation together with the analysis of the programmes outlined in a project to determine its viability, costs, resources requirements and profitability measures. Put differently, feasibility study report is a comprehensive details required for the business planning process. According to [7], feasibility study report communicates project's potentials and the liabilities associated with it within a given period. The report provides all the necessary guides for plan preparation from initiation to project execution. Furthermore, it gives direction to rational decision-making and provides whether or not to undertake the business. It also pertinent to note that no known fixed approach(es) to define feasibility study report exists. However, a good feasibility study report must be detailed, comprehensive and clear enough to assist the entrepreneur in making the right business decision.

## 9. Features of a good feasibility study

A good feasibility report must be able to highlight the following:

- Provides the foreground information for the business plan
- It contains market details in the study report
- It reflects on technical details in the study report
- It consists of detail financial implication analysis in report
- We will now discuss each of them:

i. **Background information**: the feasibility study report should contain basic information about the project such as the name of the enterprise; location details, a brief description of the project, the business history, nature of business, organisational type and the organogram showing decision hierarchy.

ii. **Market study**: this should include general market information, demand/supply analysis, competitive position, and the marketing programmes together with sales projection as appropriate.

iii. **Technical study**: this must include the description of the product to be produced, the market process, business size and production schedules. It should also describe the machinery and equipment layout with a comparative note for alternative in terms of cost, and reliability. More so, a mention of location, facilities layout for the production process, labour, utilities and raw materials in the plan is paramount.

iv. **Financial analysis**: the financial analysis component of the business plan deals with say, 5 years financial projection for an existing business; detail costs and earning from the business to evaluate rate of returns; and, fund sourcing for a new project. It is also part of financial analysis to take into account, the initial requirements, pre-operation cash-flow and financial projection for new projects, whilst consolidating the existing ones. In a nutshell, the overall financial appraisal need to reflect the total initial capital investment and recurrent expenses; projection of income flow with profit profile indications; cash-flow and rate of returns; as well as the capital needs of the business intent.

On note of these backdrop discussions, agribusiness value-chain actors should bear in mind the facts that feasibility study report is not synonymous to 'business plan'. Indeed, both terms are related but should not be mistaken to mean the same. Whilst 'business plan' is a statement describing what is to be done, how feasible or viable is it; the feasibility study explicitly conveys the viability of a business after data gathering and analysis, it comes up with a report, which serves as input for deciding the structure of a business plan. This means feasibility study precedes business plan as raw material.

## 10. Writing a good business plan

After the feasibility study report, the planner gets the clue for creating the business plan; s/he has what it takes to write a good business plan. With the relevant information at hand, investors understand how to handle the what, how, where and when questions components of the plan. Therefore, agribusiness planner should enlists all the activities in each decision area of the business operational functions, what is to be produce, market, finance and workforce of the business venture. Thus, various elements expected of a good business plan comprise:

i. **The purpose of the plan**: this help to define the nature and the needs of the society. This is where the question, 'what to produce' comes in. agribusiness value-chains actors must focus on the consumers' needs, build them in the product to satisfy those needs; otherwise, the resources expended becomes a mere waste. Under the purpose of a business plan, the vision and mission of the business investors are expressed articulately. The vision entails seeing the opportunities as a motivation for going into the business. Whilst the mission entails the unique statement of the aims for venturing into the enterprise, amidst many other strategic alternatives. Take a livestock farming for instance, the vision will be to provide the chickens and/or eggs needs of the consumers; whilst the mission is to make profit and create micro employments in the society.

ii. **The business objectives**: every business intent has certain objectives to achieve through articulate business plan. A good business objective must be SMART, that is, it should be specific, measurable, achievable, reliable, and time bound.

iii. **The business scope**: the scope as used here refers to the description of the key operations in the business. They include the product(s) line and sizes; the product's alternatives or substitutes; the product's pricing and customers' services; and, the departmentalisation or segmentation of the productive units.

iv. **Production plans**: this refers to the statements of intent on the chosen product(s) with various elements like what to produce; product nature, in terms of quality, availability, durability and affordability; production method(s); plant with equipment requirements; sources of raw materials; site location and facilities layouts; financial analysis and budgeting; plant and facilities maintenance; and risks mitigations.

v. **Marketing management plan**: this plan involves selecting the appropriate markets to serve, knowing your customers (KYC); understand the demand patterns and competitive trends; the product pricing policy; and, the promotion and market channels i.e. advertising modes like online, radio, television, social media, newspapers and magazines.

vi. **Staffing and workflows plan**: this segment largely focus on the organisational structure(s) to be adopted; the workforce plans; the sourcing and mode recruitments; the manpower training and development; and, the manpower appraisal, motivations and general welfares.

vii. **Finance plans**: this plan specifies allocation of funds among business subunits. Agribusiness investors must keep in mind the needs for proper and efficient allocation of scarce financial resources of the enterprise. Since finance is the pivot of every business, agribusiness investors should note that financial failure could spell dome for the attainment of the set goals of the business venture.

## 11. Conclusions

This chapter provides a guide for synthesising planning and entrepreneurial skills to help famers, micro investors, and local authorities to engage in small-scale agribusiness value-chains in Nigeria. It provides alternatives business strategic options for harnessing agribusinesses potentials, ranging from production, distribution, processing of agricultural products to service integration in such a manner to convert agricultural outputs for regular and timely supply of domestic and international needs. More so, this chapter help in ameliorating the current outcry for economic diversification to generate employment for teaming youths in Nigeria. Indeed, most agribusiness investors in Nigeria, experience failure due to the dearth of requisite business planning skills for the survival and growth of small-scale agribusiness value chains in the face of modern realities. Thus, this brief provides literal support for the concerted efforts of government to boost the agriculture sector as a viable alternative to over reliance on oil sector and to meet up the challenges of growth and development posed by global economic meltdown.

## 12. Recommendations

This chapter is recommended for use as reference material for current and prospective small-scale agribusiness investors to brings benefits such as risk reduction, cost savings, and high income generation through combination of known production planning and business management skills. This brief adopts discursive taxonomy, interpolating elicited facts from available literature, couples with the knowledge of on-the-job-experience to promote and support the development of businesses strategy for the transformation of the agricultural sector value-chains in Nigeria.

## Author details

Mustapha Momoh[1]*, Caroline Aturu-Aghedo[2] and Nana Usman Bature[3]

1 Department of Business Administration, University of Maiduguri, Borno State, Nigeria

2 Department of Business Administration, National Open University of Nigeria (NOUN), Abuja, Nigeria

3 Department of Business Administration, University of Abuja, Nigeria

*Address all correspondence to: tafamomoh@unimaid.edu.ng

## References

[1] Olagunju FI, Adeyemo R. Evaluation of the operational performance of the Nigerian Agricultural Credit Cooperative and Rural Development, (NACRDB) South-Western Nigeria. International Journal of Agricultural Economics and Rural Development (IJAERD9). 2008;**1**(1):53-67

[2] UNDP. Sustainable Development Goals. United Nations Development Programme. 2006. Available from: https://www.undp.org/content/undp/en/home/librarypage/corporate/undp_in_action_2006.html

[3] SMEDAN. Survey Report on Micro, Small and Medium Enterprises (MSMEs) in Nigeria: 2010 National MSME collaborative Survey. Available from: http://smedan.gov.ng/images/collaborative%20survey%20report.smedan-nbs.pdf

[4] Otiti OG. Essays on Recent Issues in the Nigerian Financial System. Lagos: CIBN Press Limited; 2007

[5] Pilon A. 50 Small Agricultural Business Ideas. 2019. Available from: www.smallbiztrends.com/2016/12/agricultural-business

[6] Ubom EE. Entrepreneurship, Small and Medium Enterprises: Theory, Practice & Policies. Lagos: Sendina Limited; 2006

[7] Nwoye M. Small business enterprises - How to start and succeed. In: Benin City, Benin Social Series for Africa. Enlarge Edition. 1994

Section 3

# Livestock Production

Chapter 7

# Do Rural Livestock Farmers Have Knowledge of Organic Livestock Farming Practices? Lesson from Southeast Nigeria

*Orgu Kenneth Chima, Chukwu Andy Onyema, Onubuogu Gilbert Chinedu and Esiobu Nnaemeka Success*

## Abstract

At global level, the use of inorganic feeds, veterinary drugs amongst others can significantly increase farm output in various livestock production systems. However, in recent times, quality-conscious consumers are increasingly seeking environmentally safe and chemical-residue free healthy livestock foods which organic production methods are said to ensure. Livestock Organic farming can offer promising opportunities for ensuring safe food, environmental sustainability, high livestock yield and income. Incidentally, empirical evidence on present discourse is still relatively very little. Although, a significant contribution has been made by various scholars, regrettably, these studies did not dwell on organic livestock practices and their knowledge level in South-east, Nigeria. Therefore, this presents a dearth in research and became increasingly pertinent that the study was systematically undertaken. A multistage and purposive random sampling procedure was used in the selection of 504 respondents who are organic livestock farmers. Data collected was analyzed using mean score analysis. Result shows that farmers had knowledge on practices of extensive system of livestock/poultry farming ($\bar{X}$=3.49); provision of natural air ($\bar{X}$=3.50); provision of natural water sprinkling during hot weather ($\bar{X}$=3.50); rearing animal without antibiotics ($\bar{X}$=3.56); and treating injured animals organically ($\bar{X}$=3.48) among others. Incidentally, majority of the livestock farmers lacked knowledge of how to induce ovulation for animals without drugs ($\bar{X}$=1.88). The inducement of ovulation for farm animals is one of the livestock organic methods used in forcing farm animals to come on heat/ovulation for quick multiplication. This method is harmful both for the animal an eventual consumer. Therefore, it is necessary that extension agents who are subject matter specialist (SMS) in livestock organic farming educate farmers on how to induce ovulation to farm animals organically with support from the government and farmers cooperative membership resources as these would significantly reduce harmful drugs injected to animal for quick ovulation and preserve the life span of the animal and consumers of the animal.

**Keywords:** Livestock, Organic Farming, Likert Scale Type, Rural farmers, and South-east, Nigeria

## 1. Introduction

Globally and particularly across Nigeria, current food production system may produce impressive quantities, but the health and environmental costs it brings have continued to demonstrates its limits [1, 2]. Organic farming provides basis for maintaining environmental goods and services at the farm level. According to [3] organic farming promotes ecological resilience, improved biodiversity, healthy management of farms and the surrounding environment, and builds on community knowledge and strength. It is therefore on this backdrop that organic farming is steadily gaining popularity all over the world and has continued to receive increasing support from government and the private sector [4, 5]. Therefore, from the researchers view, organic livestock farming is a system that rears, processes and preserves livestock without any form of chemical such as feed additives, growth, ovulation and appetite inducement among others. Livestock produce from organic farming is always one-hundred percent (100%) organic and un-denatured. In addition, rural famers can be seen as farmers living in the rural areas, most of them have low level of education, low access to information, their major occupation is subsistence farming with low farm size and farm input. They are also generally characterized by poverty, poor health condition and poor standard of living. For the purpose of the present study rural livestock farmers rear livestock, keep poultry, and engage in other wild animal hunting among others. Moreover, livestock organic farming production can offer promising opportunities for ensuring safe food, environmental sustainability, high livestock yield and income. Incidentally, empirical evidence on the present discourse is still relatively very scarce. Although, a significant contribution has been made by various scholars [6–8], regrettably, these studies did not dwell on organic livestock practices and their knowledge level in South-east Nigeria. Therefore, this presents a dearth in research and became increasingly pertinent that the study was systematically undertaken.

## 2. Methodology

The study was conducted in South-East, Nigeria. South-East comprised of five states, namely, Abia, Anambra, Ebonyi, Enugu and Imo (**Figure 1**). It has an estimated land mass of 32,610 $km^2$ and a population of 22,583,076 [9]. South-East lies between longitude $2^{\circ}61^{1}$ and $6^{0}.32^{1}$ East and latitudes $6^{\circ}74^{1}$ and $8^{\circ}15^{1}$ North of Equator with the mean annual temperature ranges from 21.6°C to 32.4°C while the annual rainfall ranges from 720 mm to 1440 mm in the rainforest region [10, 11]. The State has good climatic condition suitable for livestock farming and a good proportion of the population are essentially livestock farmers. A multistage and purposive random sampling procedure was used in the selection of respondents who are involved in organic livestock farmers. Firstly three (3) States namely Abia Ebonyi and Enugu were randomly selected from the five (5) geopolitical zone of South-East, Zone of Nigeria. Secondly, three Local Government Areas (LGAs) were purposively selected from each of selected States giving a total of nine (9) local government areas for the study. Purposive sampling was used to select only farmers who are practicing mainly organic farming. Thirdly, three (3) communities was purposively selected from each of the nine (9) selected LGAs based on the concentration of organic farmers to give a total of twenty-seven (27) communities. Finally, a stratified random sampling technique was used to select fourteen (14) livestock farmers from each of the 27 selected communities to give a total sample size of five-hundred and four (504) livestock farmers for the study. The list of livestock farmers in the communities, which forms the sample frame, was obtained

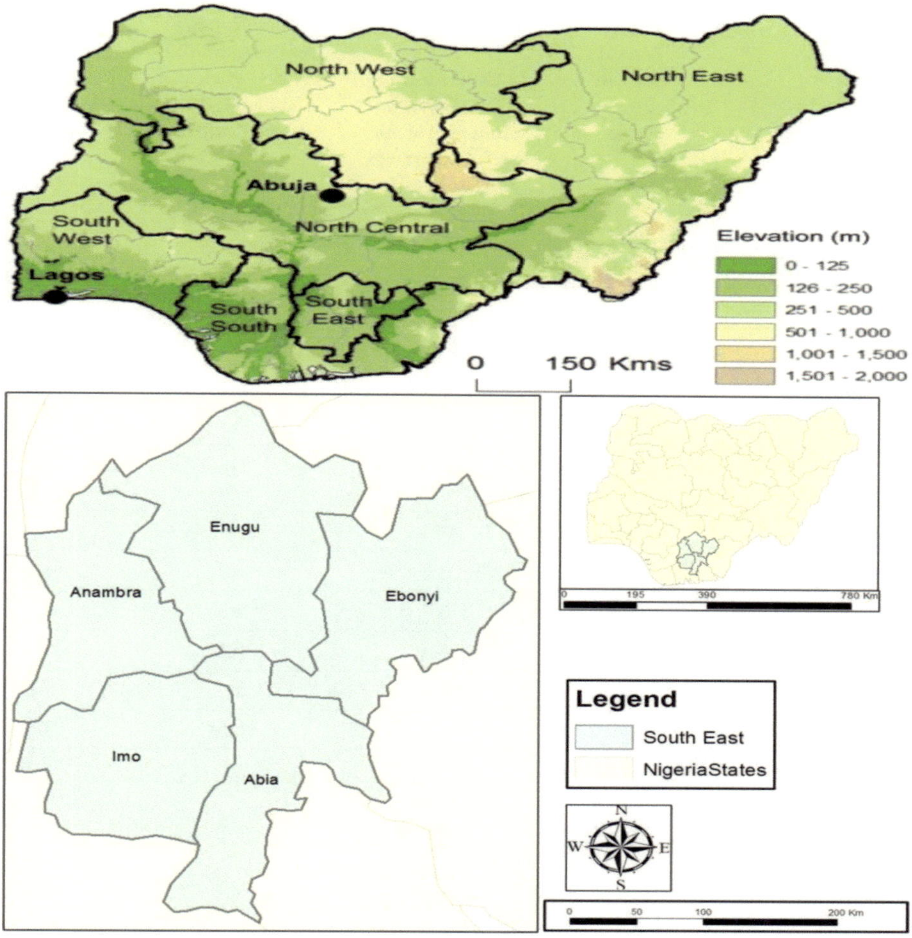


**Figure 1.**
*Map of Nigeria showing the study area.*

from the zonal extension agents of each of the State Agricultural Development Programme in the selected States. Data collected were analyzed using likert scale type. A well structured questionnaire was the main tool for data collection. Data collected were analyzed using likert scale type. The weighted mean was given below as follows:

$$X_w = \frac{\sum_{j=1}^{5} ni(5i)}{n}$$

Where Xw = Weighted Mean Score.

n = No: of respondents.

The various attributes were rated in a 4- point likert scale type of questions of Very High Knowledge (VHK) (4); High Knowledge (HK) (3); Moderate Knowledge (MK) (2) and No Knowledge (NK) (1). Using the method of mean score analysis, a discriminatory mean of 2.50 was produced. The mean value of each attribute equal to or above ($\bar{x} = \geq 2.50$) was regarded as an accepted decision while attributes with mean value less than ($\bar{x} = \leq 2.50$) was regarded as a rejected decision (**Table 1**).

| States in South-east | Agricultural Zone of Selected South east State | Total Number of Local Government Area Selected from each of the agricultural zone in South east | Total Number of Communities Selected from each of the agricultural zone in South east | Total Number of Farmers selected per community Livestock |
|---|---|---|---|---|
| **a. Abia** | Ohafia | 3 | 3x3 | 4x14 |
| **State 1** | Umuahia | 3 | 3x3 | 4x14 |
| | Aba | 3 | 3x3 | 4x14 |
| **Sub-total** | **03** | **09** | **27** | **168** |
| **b. Ebonyi** | Ebonyi-South, | 3 | 3x3 | 4x14 |
| **State 2** | Ebonyi-North | 3 | 3x3 | 4x14 |
| | Ebonyi-Central | 3 | 3x3 | 4x14 |
| **Sub-total** | **03** | **09** | **27** | **168** |
| **c. Imo** | Orlu | 3 | 3x3 | 4x14 |
| **State 3** | Owerri | 3 | 3x3 | 4x14 |
| | Okigwe | 3 | **3x3** | 4x14 |
| **Sub-total** | **03** | **09** | **27** | **168** |
| Aggregate Total | 15.00 | 27.00 | 81.00 | 504 |

*Source: Field Survey Data, 2019.*

**Table 1.**
*Sampling and sample proportion for the study.*

## 3. Results and discussion

### 3.1 Socio-economic characteristics of livestock farmers

Results in **Table 2**, showed that majority (58.53%) of the farmers fell within the age bracket of 41–50 years. The average age was 44.00 years. The farmers are still young and in an active age. Younger farmers are modern, innovative, full of physical vigor and ever-ready to try new technology faster than their older counterpart in organic farming practices. Additionally, younger farmers are also ready mentally and physically to engage in farming activities in a bid to alleviating poverty and becoming more self-reliant than their older counterpart. The finding is in agreement with the study of [7] who pointed-out that younger farmers are more involved in farming activities than older farmers in South-east Nigeria and that older farmers are not always enthusiastic about new farm technologies, especially if the benefits are not expected in the near future, but at the same time, farmers with advanced age are associated with more experience. **Table 2**, also indicates that greater proportion (61.30%) of the farmers were males. The finding implies that both sex are involved in organic farming activities but males were more in number than females in the area. This is true and could be attributed to the fact that male seems to have more access to agricultural productive inputs such as farmland, economic crops, agricultural extension services and farm credit than female in the area. Furthermore, the high number of male could also be associated to the fact than male have more physical energy to withstand the stress and strain involved in organic farming activities than female in the area. The result is

| Age (Years) | Frequency | Percentage (%) | Mean (X) |
|---|---|---|---|
| 21–30 | 8 | 1.58 | |
| 31–40 | 49 | 9.72 | |
| 41–50 | 295 | 58.53 | |
| 51–60 | 108 | 21.42 | |
| 61–70 | 32 | 6.34 | |
| 71–80 | 12 | 2.38 | |
| **Total** | **504** | **100.00** | **44.00 years** |
| **Sex** | **Frequency** | **Percentage (%)** | |
| Male | 309 | 61.30 | |
| Female | 195 | 38.69 | |
| **Total** | **504** | **100.0** | |
| **Educational Level** | **Frequency** | **Percentage (%)** | |
| No formal education | 16 | 3.174 | |
| Primary | 161 | 31.94 | |
| Secondary | 291 | 57.73 | |
| Tertiary | 36 | 7.14 | |
| **Total** | **504** | **100.00** | **13.00 years** |
| **Marital Status** | **Frequency** | **Percentage (%)** | |
| Married | 270 | 53.57 | |
| Single | 157 | 31.15 | |
| Widowed | 54 | 10.71 | |
| Divorced | 23 | 4.56 | |
| **Total** | **504** | **100.0** | |
| **Farming Experience** | **Frequency** | **Percentage (%)** | |
| 01–10 | 15 | 2.97 | |
| 10–19 | 34 | 6.74 | |
| 20–30 | 284 | 56.34 | |
| 31–40 | 101 | 20.03 | |
| 41–50 | 59 | 11.70 | |
| 51–60 | 11 | 2.18 | |
| **Total** | **504** | **100.00** | **29.00 years** |
| **Household Size (Number of Persons)** | **Frequency** | **Percentage (%)** | |
| 1–2 | 3 | 0.59 | |
| 3–4 | 14 | 2.78 | |
| 5–6 | 29 | 5.78 | |
| 7–8 | 124 | 24.60 | |
| 9–10 | 222 | 44.04 | |
| 11–12 | 101 | 20.03 | |
| 13–14 | 11 | 2.18 | |
| **Total** | **504** | **100.00** | **8.00 persons** |

| Age (Years) | Frequency | Percentage (%) | Mean (X) |
|---|---|---|---|
| **Membership of Cooperatives** | **Frequency** | **Percentage (%)** | |
| Member | 398 | 78.96 | |
| Non-member | 106 | 21.03 | |
| **Total** | **504** | **100.0** | |
| **Number of Visit** | **Frequency** | **Percentage (%)** | |
| Not at all | 147 | 29.67 | |
| Once in a fortnight | 283 | 56.15 | |
| Once in a month | 47 | 9.32 | |
| Twice in a year | 23 | 4.56 | |
| Once in a year | 4 | 0.79 | |
| **Total** | **504** | **100.0** | **2.0 times per month** |
| **Access to Farm Credit** | **Frequency** | **Percentage (%)** | |
| Access | 401 | 79.56 | |
| No-access | 103 | 20.44 | |
| Total | 504 | 100.0 | |
| **Farm Size (Herds)** | **Frequency** | **Percentage (%)** | |
| Poultry | 493* | 97.81 | |
| Pig | 382* | 75.79 | |
| Goat | 131* | 25.99 | |
| Sheep | 73* | 14.48 | |
| Cattle | 21* | 4.16 | |
| **Annual Farm Income (N)** | **Frequency** | **Percentage (%)** | |
| 100,000-200,000 | 13 | 2.58 | |
| 200,001-300,000 | 36 | 7.14 | |
| 300,001-400,000 | 28 | 5.56 | |
| 400,001-500,000 | 23 | 4.56 | |
| 600,001-700,000 | 74 | 14.70 | |
| 700,001-800,000 | 96 | 19.05 | |
| 800,001-900,000 | 223 | 44.25 | |
| 900,001-1,000,000 | 11 | 2.18 | |
| **Total** | **504** | **100.0** | **N860,700.00 (2,259.77USD)** |

**Multiple Responses were recorded; Source: Field Survey Data, 2020.*
*2.0 Knowledge Level of Farmers on Livestock Organic Farming Practices.*

**Table 2.**
*Socio-economic characteristics of livestock farmers.*

in line with the findings of [12] who reported that males constituted the greater proportion of those involved in farming activities in South-East, Nigeria. **Table 2** also shows that majority (57.73%) had secondary education. The mean education level was 13.00 years and equivalent to secondary school education. The finding indicates that approximately 96.83% of the farmers had trainings in formal educational institutions which no doubt increases their literacy levels in understanding the importance of organic farming. It is also expected that the higher level of education would contribute significantly to decision making regarding the appropriate use of organic farming practices in the area. Additionally, exposure to higher level of education is positively and significantly related to knowledge, understanding and use of organic farming practices among farmer. The finding is supported by the study of [13] who pointed the need for education in increasing farmers knowledge in order to facilitate the organic farming transition process. The study also shares view with the finding of [14] who asserted that higher education correlates positively with understanding, use and evaluation of new organic farming practices. Marital status is presented in **Table 2**. It shows that greater proportions (53.57%) of the farmers were married. This is an indication that married individual were more involved in organic farming activities in South-east Nigeria than their other counterpart. This could be as a result that married farmers tends to have access to farmland, economics trees, labour from households and access to farm credit. This finding supports the work of [15] who opined that married farmers tend to have easy access to production variables such as land and large family size which are traditionally owned and provided by household heads (husbands) to compliment family labour, reduce the cost of hired labour and improve their production. Farming experience is computed in **Table 2** and it revealed that higher proportion (56.34%) of the farmers had between 20 and 30 years of farming experience. The mean farming experience was 29.00 years. This implies that the farmers were experienced and may have been practicing several organic farming methods in the area. Having experience is one of the most useful managerial resources to organic farming. The finding is strengthened by the study of [16] who reported that experience in agribusiness enhances performance, decision making, better knowledge of climatic conditions and improve efficient use of productive resources. The result of the farmers distribution based on household size is compiled in **Table 2**. It shows that approximately 44.04% of the farmers had household size of between 9-10persons. The mean household size was 8.0 persons. This shows the farmers had large households and it is significant advantage in farming. It is expected that the very moderate household size of the farmers would serve as a source of labour in practice of several organic farming methods in the area. This findings support the result of [17] who reported that large household size is a proxy to labour availability, ensure ease allocation of resources and reduce the cost of hired labour. **Table 2** shows that greater proportion (78.96%) of the farmers in the area belong to one form of cooperative society or the other. Understanding the important of cooperative society in farming is not expected to be a challenge to the farmers in the area. Farmers that belong to cooperative society have access to relevant and up-to-date information on organic farming, farm credit and exchange of labour. The finding is supported by the result of [18] who argued that the more active the farmers are in their involvement in the farmer association, the more information of farm activities carried out and agricultural input distribution they have compared to those who do not join the association. The result of farmers distribution based on extension contact is presented in **Table 2**. It indicates that reasonable proportions (56.15%) of the farmers were visited once in a fortnight. The mean number of visits per month was 2.0. This shows that the farmers had low extension contact which may not support development of use of organic farming methods. The study of [19] asserted that extension contact promote knowledge of farmers on modern farming methods which improves their production and standard of living. **Table 2** also shows that greater proportion (79.56%) of farmers in the area had access to farm credit. This could be one of the most important factors in organic farming as majority of farmers have access to credit facilities to ensure easy purchase of farm input and expansion of farm. The study of [20] opined that the coefficient of access to farm credit was positive and significantly related to the improved production of farmers. The result of livestock farmers distribution based on farm size is displayed in **Table 2**. It shows that majority (97.81%) of the farmers in the study area were involved in poultry farming. Additionally, poultry sector in Nigeria accounts for about 58.2% of overall livestock production as it offers the nippiest profit to investment expenditures in livestock production enterprise (21). Finally, **Table 2**, it indicates that majority (44.25%) of the farmers in the study

| S/No | Livestock organic farming practices | VHK | HK | MK | NK | Mean($\bar{x}$) (≥2.50) | SD | Decision |
|---|---|---|---|---|---|---|---|---|
| 1 | Knowledge of extensive system of livestock farming | 294 (58.33) | 164 (32.54) | 44 (8.73) | 2 (0.40) | 3.49 | 0.81 | Accepted |
| 2 | Knowledge of provision of natural air | 330 (65.48) | 106 (21.03) | 60 (11.90) | 8 (1.59) | 3.50 | 0.76 | Accepted |
| 3 | Knowledge of provision of natural water sprinkling during hot weather | 272 (53.97) | 208 (41.27) | 18 (3.57) | 6 (1.19) | 3.48 | 0.66 | Accepted |
| 4 | Knowledge of rearing animal without antibiotics | 326 (64.68) | 134 (26.59) | 42 (8.33) | 2 (0.40) | 3.56 | 0.89 | Accepted |
| 5 | Knowledge of treating injured animals without drugs | 302 (59.92) | 146 (28.97) | 52 (10.32) | 4 (0.80) | 3.50 | 0.85 | Accepted |
| 6 | Knowledge of feeding animals without feed inducement | 334 (66.27) | 98 (19.44) | 64 (12.70) | 16 (3.17) | 3.52 | 0.87 | Accepted |
| 7 | Knowledge of inducing ovulation for animals without drugs | 18 (3.57) | 22 (4.37) | 340 (68.25) | 124 (24.60) | 1.88 | 0.14 | Rejected |
| 8 | Knowledge of allowing animals give birth naturally without drug inducement | 360 (71.43) | 96 (19.05) | 38 (7.54) | 10 (1.98) | 3.60 | 0.79 | Accepted |
| 9 | Knowledge of animal feeding using 100% organic feeds | 262 (51.98) | 200 (39.68) | 24 (5.56) | 14 (2.78) | 3.41 | 0.67 | Accepted |
| 10 | Knowledge of use of purely local breed of livestock | 338 (67.06) | 110 (21.82) | 44 (8.73) | 12 (2.38) | 3.51 | 0.76 | Accepted |

*Discriminatory index: Cut off point $\bar{x}$≥2.50 Accepted; $\bar{x}$≤2.50 is Rejected; *Figures in parenthesis are percentage; Field Survey Data, 2020.*
*Keys; VHK: Very High Knowledge; HK: High Knowledge; MK: Moderate Knowledge; NK: No Knowledge; SD: Standard Deviation.*

**Table 3.**
*Knowledge level of farmers on livestock organic farming practices.*

*DOI: http://dx.doi.org/10.5772/intechopen.99961*

area had an annual farm income of between N800,001–900,000. The mean annual farm income was N860,700.00 (2,259.77USD) while monthly farm income was estimated to be N 71, 725.00. This is relatively high and above the Nigeria Monthly National Minimum wage of N30,000.00. This is relatively high income could be attributed to farmers' practice of organic farming. It also shows an encouraging income realized from the practice of organic farming. The study of reported that farmers with higher farm income will make better decision, use necessary productive inputs, realize huge yield/output and be more relatively efficient than their counterparts who have low farm income.

Result of farmers distribution based on level on knowledge of livestock organic farming practices is displayed in **Table 3**. The various attributes were rated in a 4- point likert scale type of questions of Very High Knowledge (VHK) (4); High Knowledge (HK) (3); Moderate Knowledge (MK) (2) and No Knowledge (NK) (1). Using the method of mean score analysis, a discriminatory mean of 2.50 was produced. The mean value of each attribute equal to or above ($\bar{x}= \geq 2.50$) was regarded as an accepted decision while attributes with mean value less than ($\bar{x}= \leq 2.50$) was regarded as a rejected decision. The values of standard deviation (SD) denote the degree of variation in the responses of the farmers. The standard deviation value which ranged from 0.60 and above indicated that farmers were in agreement in their level of knowledge of organic farming practices. Additionally, all the items were rated high and had an acceptable overall discriminatory score ($\bar{x}= \geq 2.50$) expect the attribute of having Knowledge of inducing ovulation for animals without drugs ($\bar{x}= \leq 1.46$) and Knowledge of use of purely local breed of livestock ($\bar{x}= \leq 1.76$) which had a low acceptance and poor rating. The low level of knowledge and acceptability of the first attribute may be due to lack of knowledge of the farmers to successfully induce ovulation without drugs in farm animal. It encompasses practices like administration of hormone to non-use of biostimulation. In a similar way, farmers poor knowledge of use of purely local breed of livestock could be attributed to the fact that Nigeria local breed (chick, goat, or sheep) are usually small in size, process less meat, egg and grows slowly. Although the study of [6] reported that indigenous poultry species represent valuable resources for livestock development because their extensive genetic diversity allows for rearing of poultry under varied environmental conditions, providing a range of products and functions. Thus, great genetic resources embedded in the indigenous poultry await full exploitation that will provide basis for genetic improvement and diversification to produce breeds that are adapted to local conditions for the benefit of farmers and still less prefer to exotic breed by livestock farmers.

n = 504.

## 4. Conclusion and recommendation

Conclusively, result revealed that farmers have knowledge of the following practices extensive system of livestock/poultry farming; provision of natural air; treating injured animals without drugs; treating injured animals without drugs; provision of natural water sprinkling during hot weather; rearing animal without antibiotics; animal feeding using 100% organic feeds among other various livestock farmers possesses in livestock organic farming. Incidentally, majority of the livestock farmers have low knowledge of how to induce ovulation for animals without drugs.

## Recommendation

Therefore, the study recommends that government effort should focus on intensifying more knowledge building of farmers on organic livestock practices through strengthened agricultural extension service system. This would not only improve farmers' practice of organic livestock production but also increase their income, standard of living and reduction of health and environmental hazard associated with the use of inorganic farming in the area.

## Appreciation

We sincerely thank all those who helped us in data collation, entry, data cleaning, data coding and analysis. Many thanks to our Field volunteers. God bless you all immensely.

## Author details

Orgu Kenneth Chima, Chukwu Andy Onyema, Onubuogu Gilbert Chinedu and Esiobu Nnaemeka Success*
Department of Agricultural Economics, Extension and Rural Development Imo State University Owerri, Nigeria

*Address all correspondence to: esiobunnaemekasuccess@gmail.com

## References

[1] International Federation of Organic Agriculture Movement (IFOAM) (2020), Global Organic Agriculture: Continued Growth. BioFacch World Organic Trade Fair 2018 in Nurenberg, Germany

[2] Esiobu, N.S; Onubuogu, G.C; Njoku, S.M and Nwachukwu, B.C (2020). Sustainability and Determinate of Farmers' Mitigation Strategies to Greenhouse Gases (GHGs) Emission in Rice Agric-Food System in Nigeria; IntechOpen*; DOI: http://dx.doi.org/10.5772/intechopen.93188*; Vol. 9(6);Pp:01-16

[3] Food and Agriculture Organization (FAO). (2020). Evaluating The Potential Of Organic Agriculture ;http://www.fao.org/3/AC116E/ac116e05.htm

[4] World Bank, (2018). 4th Global Economic Update: Overcoming Constraints in the Manufacturing Sector: World Bank Report. Geneva, Switzerland.

[5] Esiobu, N.S (2020). How Does COVID-19 Pandemic Affect Rice Yield? Lessons from, Southeast Nigeria; *Journal of Biology, Agriculture and Healthcare;* Vol.10, No.15, Pp:38-56; DOI: 10.7176/JBAH/10-15-06

[6] Ajayi , F.O (2010). Nigerian Indigenous Chicken: A Valuable Genetic Resource for Meat and Egg Production. *Asian Journal of Poultry Science, 4: 164-172.*

[7] Anugwa, I and O. B.Nwobodo (2020). Assessment of Crop Farmer's Use of Organic Farming Practices in Enugu State, Nigeria; *Journal of Applied Sciences* ; Vol:3(2); Pp:4-12; DOI: 10.3923/jas.2020.83.90

[8] Ngereza, A and E. Pawelzik (2016). Constraints and opportunities of organic fruit production in Tanzania; *International Journal of Agricultural Policy and Research Vol.4 (4),* pp. 67-78

[9] Nigeria Population Commission (NPC) (2006). Nigeria Population Commission, *Nigeria Federal Government Initiative of individual head count by gender. Spread, State by State*, In: MOFINEWS; (accessed 28 February, 2016).Jan-Feb,2007, 6(3):Nigeria.

[10] Nigerian Meteorological Agency (NiMET) (2018). "Drought and Flood Monitoring in South East Bulletin". Retrieved from www .nimet.gov.ng 25 October, 2018

[11] National Bureau of Statistics (NBS) (2007). National Bureau of Statistics Official Gazette (FGP 71/52007/2,500(OL24)*: Legal Notice on Publication of the Details of the Breakdown of the National and State Provisional Totals, 2006 Census.* www.nigerianstat.gov.ng (accessed 28 February, 2016)

[12] Anyikwa, C.F, E. C.Ikechukwu, P. C. Anunobi, O.J Umeh, O.S Anyawu (2019). Analysis of Resource Management Among Male and Female Cassava Farmers in Fadama III (AF) in Anambra State, Nigeria. *International Journal of Agricultural Economics.* Vol. 4, No. 6, pp. 259-266. doi: 10.11648/j.ijae.20190406.12

[13] Joy, R. P, Y.P Lin and R.F. Wunderlich (2019). Analyzing Opinions on Sustainable Agriculture: Toward Increasing Farmer Knowledge of Organic Practices in Taiwan-Yuanli Township; Sustainability; Vol.14, No. 2, 11-21

[14] Adebiyi , A , L.S. Olabisi, R. Richardson , L. Saweda, O. Liverpool-Tasie and K. Delate (2020). Drivers and Constraints to the Adoption of Organic Leafy Vegetable Production in Nigeria: A Livelihood Approach; Sustainability;

Vol(23)12, 96-109; doi:10.3390/su12010096

[15] Onubuogu, G,C and N.S Esiobu (2020). Determinants of allocative (pricing) efficiency of cassava farms in Imo State, Nigeria; *Journal of Agriculture and Food Sciences*; Vol 17; No 2; https://www.ajol.info/index.php/jafs/article/view/194543

[16] Osuji, N.M (2019). Determinants of Poverty Status of Cassava based Farmers in Imo State, Nigeria; *Advances in Research; 20(1): 1- 8; Article no.AIR. 50390*

[17] Eze, A.V and S.U Nwibo (2014). Economic and technical efficiency of cassava production in Ika North East Local Government Area of Delta State, Nigeria. *Journal of Development and Agricultural Economics*. 2014;6(10):429-436.

[18] Onumadu, F. N. and E.E Osahan (2014). Socio-Economic determinants of Adoption of improved rice technology by farmers in Ayamelu Local Government Area of Anambra State, Nigeria. Department of Rural Sociology and Extension, Micheal Okpara University of Agriculture. Umudike, Umuahia, Abia State, Nigeria. *Internal Journal of scientific and Technology Research*. Volume3,Issue1,; Pp:12-24

[19] Chukwu, A. O. (2013). Farmers' Perception of the Effectiveness of Extension Principles in Extension Delivery in Owerri Agricultural zone, Imo State, Nigeria. *Int. J. Appl. Res. Technol*. 2(3): 38 – 43.

[20] Esiobu, N.S (2019).Relative Efficiencies Of Resource Use Among Cassava Farmers In Imo State, Nigeria; An M.Sc Thesis Submitted To The Department Of Agricultural Economics, Extension And Rural Development, Faculty Of Agriculture And Veterinary Medicine; Imo State University, Owerri, Nigeria; In Partial Fulfillment Of The Requirement For The Award Of Master's Degree In Agricultural Economics